The Racine Drum and Bugle Corps' roots in Racine run deep and wide. Thank you for telling the story of one of Racine's finest historical assets.

—RACINE MAYOR JOHN DICKERT

Racine's HORLICK ATHLETIC FIELD

DRUMS ALONG THE FOUNDRIES

ALAN R. KARLS

THE History PRESS

Published by The History Press
Charleston, SC 29403
www.historypress.net

First published 2014

Manufactured in the United States

ISBN 978.1.62619.444.1

Library of Congress CIP data applied for.

Brothers James and William Horlick invented malted milk, the first dried milk product, in Racine in 1883 and got rich. William Horlick (1846–1936) funded many local sports teams, including two early NFL football teams. In 1919, he bought Racine's largest sports field, Wisconsin-Illinois (WI) League Park, from a defunct Class D baseball team to ensure that his various teams had a reliable place to play. He renamed it Horlick Athletic Field.

Over the next twenty years, William Horlick built a 1920s-modern, covered-bleacher baseball park, later paid for stadium-quality nightlights and then gave Horlick Field to the city. William Horlick was a lifelong philanthropist. He gave considerable land and money to build a high school that bears his name, donated beautiful riverside land that is now a park that bears his name and gave untold amounts to his community during his lifetime.

This book is dedicated to William Horlick, whose name will live as long as there is a Racine, and who gave me a place to watch my high school football games and all those great drum and bugle corps shows.

Horlick Athletic Field.

Contents

Foreword, by Steve Vickers 9
Acknowledgements 11
Introduction 13

1. The Early Years: 1919–1951 17
2. Horlick Field Develops a Reputation: 1952–1961 45
3. The Golden Years: 1962–1978 71
4. The Legend Begins: 1962 73
5. The Troopers Arrive: 1963 83
6. The Second-Best Show Ever Held in Horlick Athletic Field: 1964 93
7. The Most Corps Performances in One Year: 1965 105
8. The Fight for Finals: 1966 115
9. The Big Upset: 1967 121
10. West Coast Drum and Bugle Corps Arrive: 1968 127
11. The Must-Play Place: 1969–1978 135
12. Four Shows, Forty-four Performances, Four California Corps, Four Performances by National Champions: 1969 137
13. Three Performances by National Champions: 1970 147
14. Anaheim Kingsmen Wins by Ten: 1971 153
15. The Best Show in Horlick Athletic Field History: 1972 157
16. A Two-Drum Corps Exhibition: 1973 165
17. Twenty-three Shows in Five Years: 1974–1978 171

18. Four Contests and the National Champion: 1974 173
19. The Top Three in One Show for the Second Year in a Row: 1975 179
20. The Top Four in One Show: 1976 185
21. The Most Shows in One Year: 1977 191
22. The End of an Era: 1978 197
23. The Long Decline: 1979 and Beyond 203

Appendix 229
Some Horlick Athletic Field Facts 229
List of Horlick Athletic Field Drum and Bugle Corps Shows 230
List of Rainouts 234
Number of Times Each Corps Appeared in Horlick Athletic Field 234
Number of Wins in Horlick Athletic Field 241
Biggest Shows in Horlick Athletic Field History 243
Index 249
About the Author 255

Foreword

As a bit of a history buff on the topic of drum and bugle corps, I've had the opportunity to become aware of many things that have happened over the years since the first competition in 1921 at the American Legion National Convention in Kansas City, Missouri.

Racine has played a major part in the so-far (2014) ninety-three-year history of this movement. The Boys of '76 won their first title at the 1922 Legion championship in New Orleans, Louisiana, and, over their existence, repeated that achievement two more times in the 1920s (1923 and 1924) and placed among the top ten senior corps almost consistently until their final appearance at American Legion Nationals in 1969 at Atlanta, Georgia.

Of course, Horlick Field played a major part in the yearly development of the Boys of '76 and the other corps that called Racine home: the YMCA Kilties, Kiltie Kadets, Racine Explorer and Junior Scouts, AmbassaDears, New Day and New Dawn, among others.

Al Karls has delved into historical and newspaper records to find every shred of evidence that shows how Horlick Field showcased the top regional and national junior and senior corps at a site that thousands of fans recall with fond memories. The feeling of intimacy (members close to the stands) demonstrated the passion and excitement in the faces of countless young people and adults who graced the turf at one of the "Drums Along the Foundries" competitions over decades of performances.

This book adds to the growing documentation of why Racine, Wisconsin, was proclaimed the "Drum Corps Capital of the World." For anyone who has marched in or witnessed a drum and bugle corps event at Horlick Field, this is a must-have in your library!

Steve Vickers, Publisher
Drum Corps World, Madison, Wisconsin
www.drumcorpsworld.com

ACKNOWLEDGEMENTS

Many people helped to make this book possible. I would like to particularly thank the *Racine Journal Times*, the Racine Library, the Racine Heritage Museum and *Drum Corps World* for their records and artifacts; *Drum Corps World*, Moe Knox, Ron Da Silva, Jim Anello, Sandy House and John Schoenknecht for graciously allowing the use of their photographs; Racine mayor John Dickert and Steve Vickers of *Drum Corps World* for their kind words; and George D. Fennell for inspiration and his scholarship: some of the scores herein were found only in his books. In addition, many people gave assistance in tracking down shows and the corps in attendance, including Joe Fazzari of the Kilties organization and Ken Norman. Mike Kaufman, a former Racine Scout, Boys of '76 and member of several alumni corps, helped find corps veterans interested in offering reminiscences.

RACINE HERITAGE MUSEUM

The Racine Heritage Museum has a voluminous collection of drum and bugle corps artifacts and is a great source for anyone interested in researching drum and bugle corps history. It is also a great place to donate drum corps memorabilia. If you have materials that you would like to see preserved and shared with generations to come, consider donating to the Racine Heritage Museum.

Racine Heritage Museum
701 Main Street
Racine, WI 53403
262.636.3926

Drum Corps World

Drum Corps World has been the leading independent voice of the drum and bugle corps activity for over forty years. It gives its readers a detailed view into the important news of the day. You can obtain a free subscription to *Drum Corps World* at www.drumcorpsworld.com.

Other Racine Drum Corps History Books

George D. Fennell has produced three books on Racine drum and bugle corps history. They are filled with facts and images.

- *Racine: Drum and Bugle Corps Capital of the World*
- *We Winna Be Dauntit!—The History of the Racine Kilties*
- *The Racine American Legion Post 76 Drum and Bugle Corps*

Other Drum and Bugle Corps History Books

A History of Drum & Bugle Corps, vols. 1 and 2
Drum Corps World

Introduction

If Racine is the drum and bugle corps capital of the world, then Horlick Athletic Field is its cathedral. The site hosted drum and bugle corps performances before it was named Horlick Field in 1919, and it has been the site of multiple-unit drum and bugle corps events since at least 1931. By 1941, Horlick Field had become a revered place in which drum and bugle corps were honored to perform.

In the early 1960s, when few corps traveled and corps from other regions of the country were rarely seen, Horlick Field regularly hosted corps from Canada, Missouri, Michigan, Indiana, Ohio, Illinois, Iowa and Minnesota. St. Raphael's Golden Buccaneers of Bridgeport, Connecticut, and St. Joseph's of Batavia, New York, competed in 1962. Casper, Wyoming Troopers in 1963. Boston Crusaders and Toronto Optimists in 1964. Hutchinson, Kansas Sky Ryders and Metairie, Louisiana Stardusters in 1965. By the end of 1969, when West Coast drum and bugle corps were still rare in the Midwest, five West Coast corps—Anaheim Kingsmen; Santa Clara Vanguard; Bellevue, Washington Sentinels; Pinole Princemen; and the Velvet Knights—had performed a total of six times in Horlick Field. And the Casper, Wyoming Troopers had performed seven times.

Between 1962 and 1978, Horlick Athletic Field was a phenomenon; it hosted more drum and bugle corps shows and more drum and bugle corps than any other venue in the country. Staff and marching members alike referred to it as "the big time." Everyone knew that if you won the Horlick Field audience, you were a good corps. And if you won one of its big shows, you were a contender. As a result, drum corps from every region of the continent flocked to Horlick Field to perform and get their measure.

You would not think it to look at it.

Even in 1962, Horlick Field was an old, small stadium packed between foundries, scrap yards and old neighborhoods. Locals referred to Horlick Field drum corps shows as "Drums Along the Foundries." The field is deep inside the city on narrow neighborhood streets and is hard to find and get to. Parking is difficult. But it is in Racine.

By the 1960s, Racine was five generations deep in the drum and bugle corps activity. Racine had had German-influenced brass and drum bands since the 1840s, and from the start, local newspapers mentioned that this or that drum and bugle corps appeared at a local parade, sporting event or street paving or welcomed a dignitary at the train station and paraded him downtown. For instance, the *Racine Advocate* newspaper of July 6, 1859, reports that the American Bugle Band led a parade.

In 1964, Racine had a championship-contending senior corps, the national championship junior corps, a second junior corps that was a frequent championship finalist, an all-girl corps, three Class B and C corps and a national championship marching band, the Racine Elks Youth Band. And the Elks was often described as a drum corps with woodwinds; it looked and performed like a drum corps. In 1967, the United States Congress declared Racine the "Drum and Bugle Corps Capital of the World" in recognition of its unique place in drum corps history and for the amazing number of high-quality marching units in the city.*

All this meant that Racine had a huge, sophisticated drum corps fan base. People often remark that Racine audiences were among the most knowledgeable in the country: they knew and appreciated good corps. When a Horlick Field crowd really liked a corps, it could give the corps ear-splitting standing ovations from the beginning to the end of its performance. Many performers say that a Horlick Field show was the most exciting performance in their corps' histories. But if you weren't very good, the Horlick Field crowd would let you know that, too. When you left Horlick Field, you had a good idea of how good your corps was.

In addition to the knowledgeable audience, another factor helped make Horlick Field the exciting place it was for drum corps performers and audiences alike. In 1964, Horlick Field's thirty-nine-year-old baseball

*. For more detailed information on Racine's drum and bugle corps history, see George D. Fennell's wonderful *Racine, Drum and Bugle Corps Capital of the World.*

field configuration was replaced with a compact football field and separate baseball field. The new football field grandstands were only a few feet from the front sideline and five feet up. It put audience members right on top of the performers. They could see the eyes of the performers, and the performers saw nothing but the faces in the always-packed crowd. The redesign made Horlick Athletic Field an intimate place in which performers made personal connections with a uniquely knowledgeable and appreciative drum corps audience.

Between 1962 and 1978, Horlick Field Athletic shows were spectacular in name and quality. Many Horlick Field drum corps shows exceeded the number and quality of the units that appeared at renowned national contests such as the Dream, World Open and CYO Nationals. Year after year and several times a year, Horlick Field hosted electrifying drum and bugle corps shows filled with the best drum corps in the activity. During this period, Horlick Field was a center of the drum and bugle corps activity. Now that activity has all but forgotten it.

But it still sells beer.

Horlick Athletic Field Statistics, 1931–2013

99	drum and bugle corps shows
8	music festivals with multiple drum and bugle corps exhibitions
199	number of drum and bugle corps that appeared in Horlick Athletic Field
885+	drum and bugle corps performances in shows and music festivals*
21	times the VFW, American Legion, DCI or DCA Champion performed
2	shows that had the year's VFW and American Legion champions together in one show
2	shows that had the top four VFW/DCI finalists
5	shows that had the top three VFW/DCI finalists
4	shows that had seven national contest finalist drum and bugle corps
7	shows that had six national contest finalist drum and bugle corps

220	performances by a championship finalist drum and bugle corps
25	drum and bugle corps in largest show
2	drum and bugle corps in smallest show
4	days on which Horlick Field hosted two drum and bugle corps contests

*There were untold more exhibition units at various shows that were not recorded, and the contestants at one show are unknown.

Chapter 1

THE EARLY YEARS

1919–1951

> *W.I. League Park Is Bought by Horlick*
> *W.M. Horlick announces the purchase of the W.I. league park and the fact that it will be known in the future as the Horlick Athletic field. The grounds to the west of the park have been annexed and the foregoing title will apply to that tract as well as the park proper. They will be used for baseball, football and all other outside games.*
> —Racine Journal News, *October 18, 1919*

The first drum and bugle corps to appear on the site after William Horlick purchased the Wisconsin-Illinois League Park and renamed it Horlick Athletic Field is unknown; newspaper records are erratic, and those who would remember have long since passed. The active Racine drum and bugle corps of the time were Holy Name, Elks, Knights of Columbus, Aden Temple and an early and short-lived Boy Scout unit that was taught by members of Holy Name. A drum corps formed by Racine soldiers while serving in World War I performed sporadically under multiple names after the war until it was reorganized and formalized as the Racine Legion drum and bugle corps in 1921. Any one of these corps might have been the first drum and bugle corps to appear at the site after it was named Horlick Athletic Field on October 18, 1919.

However, it is likely that Holy Name drum and bugle corps was the first to appear in Horlick Field. It was the leading drum and bugle corps in Racine in 1919 when the site became known as Horlick Athletic Field, and the *Racine*

Racine Legion (Boys of '76) drum and bugle corps in Horlick Athletic Field, 1922 or 1923. *Racine Heritage Museum.*

Journal News reported on October 2, 1916, that Holy Name performed at a football game on the site in 1916, three years before it became known as Horlick Field:

> *Sailors Go Down to Defeat Manning Their Guns; Army Wins Game 30 to 0 ...About one thousand saw the game...in the W.-I. league park...The soldiers marched in and took their places in the grand stand led by the drum corps from the Holy Name society...most of the noise of the afternoon was created by the drum corps which performed its part manfully...After the first half was over the soldiers, again led by the drum corps, circled the field.*

The earliest record discovered that relates a drum and bugle corps to Horlick Athletic Field is from the October 20, 1921 *Racine Journal News,* which reports that the Racine Legion (Boys of '76) drum and bugle corps led a parade to a Horlick Field football game. While it can be assumed that Legion performed on the field during the game—a different account that year reported that the Legion drum corps led a parade to a game in Milwaukee against the Green Bay Packers and performed at halftime of the game—there is no account of Legion performing in Horlick Field after the October 1921 parade.

The earliest historic record found of a drum and bugle corps in Horlick Field is a grainy photocopy of a picture of the Racine Legion appearing at

The Racine Legion had its beginnings as a World War I U.S. Army drum and bugle corps formed by Racine soldiers serving in Batteries C and F, 121st Artillery, 32nd Division, nicknamed the Red Arrow Division. The members returned to Racine from France on May 20, 1919, and played together sporadically as the 32nd Division Veteran's drum and bugle corps and other names until 1921, when the group absorbed members of the Holy Name drum corps and officially organized as the Racine Legion drum and bugle corps. Racine Legion's precision, musicality and innovation set the standards against which drum and bugle corps would be judged for decades. For a detailed account of the early Racine Legion drum and bugle corps, see George D. Fennell's *The Racine American Legion Post 76 Drum and Bugle Corps*.

a football game in 1922 or 1923; the uniforms shown in the picture were worn only during those years. The picture shows the original field layout that existed before William Horlick built a "modern" baseball field and covered bleachers in 1925.

Throughout the period from 1919 to 1951, drum and bugle corps appeared at many events each year in Horlick Field as pomp and circumstance, flag raising and musical entertainment for the wide variety of events that Horlick Field hosted, including baseball, football, soccer, circuses, demolition derbies, rodeos, donkey baseball games and others. If there was a ticketed outdoor event in Racine, it was likely held at Horlick Field, and a drum corps was likely to be there.

In this early form of the drum and bugle corps activity, it could be estimated that Horlick Field hosted enough individual performances of Racine's many drum corps each year that, if put together, they would make for two good-sized drum and bugle corps shows.

Drum and bugle corps were particularly linked to the All-American Girls Professional Baseball League's Racine Belles team. Ads for games regularly listed one of the Racine drum corps as a featured attraction. The Racine Boy Scouts led parades to the field and appeared at opening day on several occasions. If you have ever seen the movie *A League of Their Own*, picture Horlick Field and a Racine drum and bugle corps. While the final game of the movie is set in a fictitious "Racine Field," the game was in reality held in Horlick Athletic Field, and one of Racine's drum and bugle corps was probably there.

The earliest record found of an event with two or more drum and bugle corps together in Horlick Field was the Racine Music Festival in 1931, at which the Racine Legion and Racine Boy drum and bugle corps performed. Racine held music festivals in Horlick Field under a variety of sponsors eight times between 1933 and 1951. Each time, two to four Racine drum corps performed in pre-festival exhibition, including the Legion, Racine Boy Scouts, Kilties, Belle City, Roma Lodge and Armenian Youth drum and bugle corps.

The first drum and bugle corps contest held in Horlick Field was the 1939 Veterans of Foreign Wars (VFW) state contest.

In 1941, Horlick Field hosted what may be the first self-sponsored drum and bugle corps show in history. Until then, all contests were either sponsored by state or county fairs and VFW and American Legion conventions or were just one part of large festivals that might also have bands, drill teams, individual performers, vocal competitions and circus acts. The American Legion held its national convention in Milwaukee in 1941, and the Racine Legion took advantage of it. Legion invited several of the corps that were to appear in Milwaukee to compete in a drum corps–only show in Horlick Field the night before the national championship contest.

World War II interrupted the growth of the drum corps activity and the development of drum corps contests. No competitions were held in Horlick Field during the war. However, Racine's drum and bugle corps continued to perform at Horlick Field during the war at various events, as witnessed by ads and newspaper accounts. The first postwar contest in Horlick Field was the American Legion State Championship in 1946.

Between the years 1946 and 1951, returning World War II veterans revitalized the drum and bugle corps activity. (At the 1946 American Legion state championship contest in Horlick Field, many returning servicemen wore their military uniforms instead of their corps uniforms during their corps' performances.) Drum and bugle corps became bigger, better trained and more professional in operation, and self-sponsored contests began to appear, including the Dream in Jersey City, New Jersey, in 1949. Horlick Athletic Field began to host regular, annual drum and bugle corps contests in 1952.

RACINE'S MUSIC FESTIVALS

A 1934 Racine music festival poster.

Racine's music festivals are examples of the events at which drum and bugle corps performed before World War II. Drum corps were just one part of a much larger musical event or, in the case of the Kenosha Roundup, an act added to a clown circus and rodeo.

The Racine Music Festival was one of the many music festivals started in the wake of the giant Chicagoland Music Festival. Chicagoland, begun in 1929, was a huge event with up to 150,000 spectators and a national radio audience. The South Milwaukee Spectacle of Music and the Cedarburg Music Festivals were other festivals spawned by Chicagoland. The Racine Scouts touted its victory at the 1935 Chicagoland Music Festival in its standard contest spiel sheet into the late 1960s.

The music festivals held in Horlick Field were:

August 12, 1931
Racine Legion (Boys of '76)..A4*
Racine Scouts

August 16, 1933
Racine Legion (Boys of '76)
Racine Scouts
Roma Lodge

July 31, 1934
Racine Legion (Boys of '76)..A10
Racine Scouts
Armenian Youth

August 5, 1936
Racine Legion (Boys of '76)
Racine Scouts
Roma Lodge
Kilties

August 12, 1937
Racine Legion (Boys of '76)
Racine Scouts
Kilties

June 4, 1940
Racine Legion (Boys of '76)
Racine Scouts
Roma Lodge
Kilties

June 24, 1941
Racine Legion (Boys of '76)
Kilties
Belle City, Racine

August 15, 1951
Racine Legion (Boys of '76)
Racine Scouts
Kilties

*Corps that performed in national championship finals contests are noted throughout this book by place taken and by contest.

- A (American Legion)
- V (VFW)
- DCA (Drum Corps Associates)
- D (Drum Corps International)

JUNE 24, 1936—HORLICK FIELD GETS NEW LIGHTS

> *Racine Belles Down Chairs In Overtime Battle, 7 To 6*
> *More than 4,000 fans attended the dedication of the new lighting system at Horlick Field, Racine, last night...Preceding the game, the Racine Legion Drum and Bugle Corps presented a ten minute drill just after William Horlick, who donated the park to the city early this year, gave the signal that turned on the park's new lighting system.*
> —Sheboygan Press, *June 25, 1936*

Horlick Field had night games before, but new stadium-quality lights were installed on June 24, 1936. The Racine Belles in this article was a Class D minor league men's baseball team, one of many semiprofessional and amateur teams that played at Horlick Field over the years and had drum corps as entertainment. William Horlick died later that year.

JUNE 24, 1939—VFW STATE CHAMPIONSHIP

> *Overseas Drum Corps Going to VFW Meet*
> *The Madison Veterans of Foreign Wars Overseas drum and bugle corps will leave Madison tomorrow morning at 6 for the state V.F.W. convention in Racine. The corps will march in the convention parade tomorrow afternoon at 3 and defend its state championship under the Horlick field*

lights at 6:30 p.m. Its opposition will be drum and bugle corps from La Crosse, Sheboygan, Milwaukee and Waukesha.
—Capital Times, *Madison, Wisconsin, June 23, 1939*

Horlick Field had stadium-quality nightlights for three years by the time of this article, and it was still news in Wisconsin. Horlick Field, under the lights, great drum and bugle corps and thousands in the audience—it was a formula that would be repeated for over seventy years.

June 24, 1939—VFW State Championship

1. Overseas Drum and Bugle Corps, Madison
2. Sheboygan
3. Janesville

Exhibition

Racine Legion (Boys of '76)..A10

La Crosse, Milwaukee and Waukesha drum corps were in the parade but were not mentioned in the newspaper account as performing in the contest.

VFW Drum, Bugle Corps Win Again
Overseas Drum and Bugle corps retained for Madison the Veterans of Foreign Wars state championship by defeating drum and bugle corps from Sheboygan, La Crosse and Janesville at Racine Saturday. Second place was awarded to the Sheboygan corps…The Overseas Drum and Bugle Corps has been state champions for four consecutive years, winning in 1936, 1937, 1938 and 1939. The musical director is Harold M. Luetscher and the drill master is W.J. Miles. A.J. Taff is president.
—Capital Times, *Madison, Wisconsin, June 26, 1939*

September 13, 1941—Racine Legion Invitational

Drum Corps Invited to Racine
…It has been decided to offer $1,325 in prizes in the drum corps and parade competitions. The drum corps contest will be held in Horlick Athletic field that night.

Prize money will be apportioned on this scale: drum corps competition, $500 for the first place corps; $300 for second place and $200 for third *place. Senior drum corps awards for the best two outfits in the parade, $75 first and $50 second; junior, $50 first and $25 second, and bands, $75 first and $50 second.*

Invitations will be extended to from five to seven drum corps which placed in the finals at the national Legion convention in 1940 to take part in the drum corps contest...Members of the participating units will be given their dinners in a large tent on the field.

—Racine Journal Times, *June 3, 1941*

The letter below attests to the respect that Racine had already earned by 1941 as a leader in the drum and bugle corps activity. While the article and letter speak of the Cudworth drum corps marching only in the parade, it also performed in the competition and took third.

Milwaukee Drum, Bugle Corps To Appear in Racine Parade

Racine American Legion Post No. 76 drew praise from a Milwaukee corps that will participate in a parade to be held Sept. 13 in connection with the pre-national convention celebration in Racine. Joseph Strdlick, president of the Cudworth post Sons of the American Legion drum corps, state champions in 1936, 1939 and 1940, wrote the following in accepting an invitation to march and play in Racine:

"We are conducting a drum corps rehearsal Friday night and ordinarily all invitations for corps appearances are held up until presented to the corps, but I feel so confident that our corps will accept that I am now typing the reply.

We, like all Legion music outfits all over the United States, have been inspired in our drum corps development by your Racine drum corps that has pioneered and led the way that has made possible the present Legion drum corps competition, which is the outstanding show that thrills thousands of persons annually and sold the public on the American Legion.

I am convinced that the present prestige the American Legion holds in the minds of the public is directly due to the many, many fine and splendid Legion musical units that are developed down through the years because of the inspiration your splendid Racine drum corps gave to every Legion post in the early days of Legion national convention parades and competition.

When I feel that we owe you men in Racine this kind of a compliment I also feel that we have got to accept your invitation to appear in your parade on Saturday, Sept. 13, and, therefore, I am taking this liberty of writing in advance and informing you that we will march. Thanks for the invitation."

—Racine Journal Times, *August 29, 1941*

Square Post Chicago; Drum and Bugle Corps
Square post drum and bugle corps of Chicago will be one of several competing for first prize of $500 in the drum corps competition to be staged by Racine post of the American Legion on Horlick Athletic field at 7:30 p.m. Saturday. This outfit, entered in the national competition in Milwaukee on Monday and looked upon as a strong contender, has been state champion of Illinois since 1936. It was organized in 1928.
—caption from the Racine Journal Times, *September 13, 1941*

SEPTEMBER 13, 1941—RACINE LEGION INVITATIONAL

Senior

1. Square Post 232, Chicago A5
2. Charles Hagestrom Post, Wisconsin Rapids
3. Bendix Aviation Post, South Bend, IN

Junior

1. Cornwall Post, Chicago A3
2. 98.5 Racine Scouts A7
3. Cudworth SAL

Exhibition

Racine Legion (Boys of '76) A8

This first drum corps–only show in Horlick Field set the stage for all other shows. It had good corps from several states, good prize money and thousands in the stands. The $500 winner's prize was still a sizable award twenty-five years later.

This was a very good show in its day. It had seven corps and four national championship contest finalists. Cornwall took third at American Legion nationals in 1940 and 1941. Cudworth took seventh in Boston in 1940 but could not compete in 1941 because it was a host city corps. And the Racine Scouts finished seventh at American Legion in 1941.

The following corps were in the preshow parade but were not mentioned as performing at the show: Appleton SAL (Americanos), Kilties, Kenosha SAL and Racine Belle City.

> *Square Post of Chicago Wins First, Drum Corps Prize*
> *Racine residents, and visiting members of the American Legion witnessed a colorful spectacle at Horlick's Athletic field Saturday night, when six Legion drum corps competed for $1,000 in cash prizes. More than 3,000 persons watched three drum and bugle corps, representing Bendix Aviation post 284, South Bend, Ind.; Square post of Chicago and the Charles Hagestrom post of Wisconsin Rapids, put on 15-minute drills under the same conditions that will prevail at the national competition in Milwaukee Tuesday, where these teams will strive for national recognition.*
>
> *Judges George Colman, Chicago; Larry Hammond; Chicago; John Lehtfer, Rochester, Minn., and Frederick Schulte, Racine, awarded first place to the Square post of Chicago. Charles Hagestrom post of Wisconsin Rapids was second, and Bendix Aviation post third. Sons of the American Legion Cudworth post of Milwaukee, and Cornwall post of Chicago,*

and Racine's Boy Scouts presented 10-minute exhibition drills, and top honors went to the snappy...Cornwall post. This corps placed third at the national convention at Boston last year, Racine Boy Scouts took second place, and the Cudworth squadron of Milwaukee placed third.
—Racine Journal Times, *September 15, 1941*

August 3, 1946—American Legion State Championship

This show is an example of the confusing classes of competition at the time. In this show, Class A was for senior, all-Legionnaire units. Auxiliary was for women's units. Sponsored was for non-Legion units sponsored by a Legion post. Junior was for units composed of children of Legionnaires, which were called "Sons of American Legion" or SAL corps. And, in this show, Out-of-State were units invited to make a bigger show.

Throughout the early years of drum and bugle corps, competitions and scoring were ad hoc and competing categories were arbitrary. A unit could perform against seniors in one contest and juniors in the next, under a wide variety of category names. Further confusing research efforts, many American Legion posts had junior and senior units, and each was often identified only by the post name, so one is never sure if the corps reported in Class A or B, Junior or other categories was the senior or junior unit.

The Racine Scouts, Kilties and Legion could not compete at this show, as Legion rules prohibited host city units from competing. A crowd of 5,400 people attended the show.

August 3, 1946—American Legion State Championship

Class A

1. River Falls Post 121

Auxiliary

1. Meuli-Kilian Unit 77 (Chippewa Falls All-girl)

Sponsored

1. Cains Post Boy Scouts (Madison Scouts)

Junior

1. Cudworth SAL
2. Appleton SAL (Americanos)

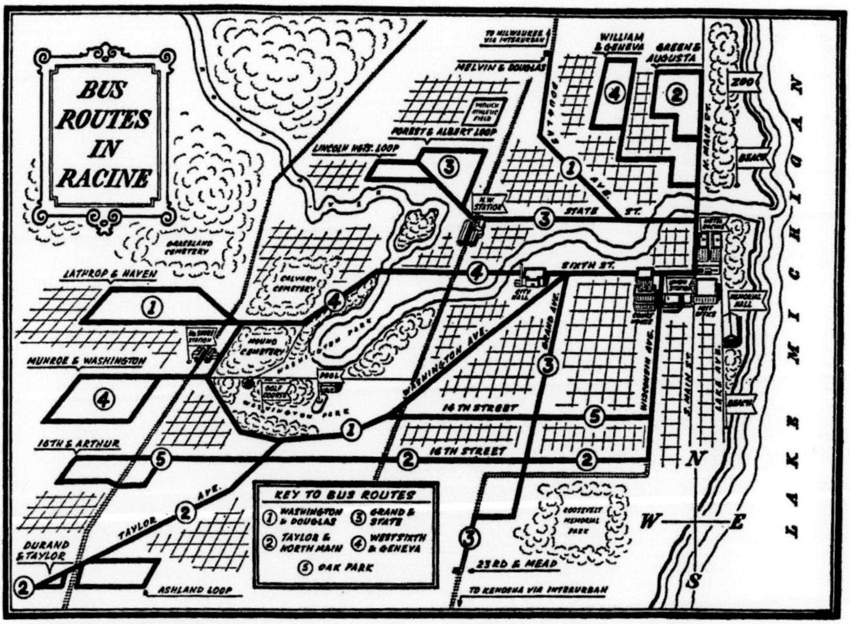

WHAT TO DO, WHERE TO GO, AND HOW TO GET THERE

A Guide to Racine for Visiting Legionnaires

HORLICK'S ATHLETIC FIELD—For the ball game Saturday Aug. 3 at 2:30 p. m. between the Racine Belles and the Grand Rapids Chicks, and for the game at 7 p. m. on Sunday Aug. 4, take the northbound GRAND-STATE bus marked "Forest-Albert" at any downtown corner and get off at Forest and Albert Sts.. Walk north. Or, take the northbound WASHINGTON-DOUGLAS bus, get off at High St. and walk west. The Drum Corps competition at Horlick Field will be held on Saturday Aug. 3d at 7:00 p. m.

FOR A GAME OF GOLF — Take the westbound WASHINGTON-DOUGLAS bus and get off at West Blvd. Walk a few steps north to Twelfth St. and then walk east on Twelfth past cemetery to the Washington Park Club House.

TO VISIT OUR ZOO — Take the northbound TAYLOR-N. MAIN bus and get off at Walton Ave.

TO GO BATHING IN LAKE MICHIGAN — Take the northbound TAYLOR-N. MAIN bus to Kewaunee and walk east.

TO GO FROM DOWNTOWN RACINE TO DOWNTOWN MILWAUKEE — Take the Milwaukee-Racine-Kenosha Interurban from the Union Station on Wisconsin Ave., a short block south of Sixth Street. Hourly service.

TO VISIT KENOSHA — Take the M.R.K. Interurban southbound. Hourly Service.

RACINE MOTOR COACH LINES

This bus company ad was for the 1946 Wisconsin American Legion Convention. Horlick Field is in the center top of the map.

Out-of-State

1. Curtis O. Reddin Post 210, Danville, IL
2. Square Post 232, Chicago
3. Gary Memorial Post 232
4. Peoria Post 2..A7
5. Melin Romer Post 728, Chicago
6. Charles Roth Post 692, Oak Park, IL

Exhibition

Rhinelander
Fond du Lac Post
Racine Legion (Boys of '76)

> *Martial Music Is Theme For Drum Corps Competition*
> *Martial Music was the theme for Saturday's American Legion drum and bugle corps competition at Horlick Athletic Field, an event that drew the largest crowd to see any event in the convention except the parade.*
>
> *The crowd filled the regular grand stand and bleacher seats on the field, besides special bleachers set up in Horlick center field and overflowed in a solid bank around the wall of the park. The marching bands paced a prescribed course across the outfield of the baseball diamond, as judges watched their every movement and judged them from the sidelines… The pageant of the marching drum and bugle corps on the field was a continuous stream of colorful uniforms, rolling drums and gleaming bugles. Uniforms varied from strict military numbers to standard Legion apparel to kilts and Spanish costumes. The music had the same range, with the Spanish costumed band, a Sons of the Legion unit from Appleton, playing, "La Paloma," "Ramona" and "Brahm's Lullaby," all in marching tempo.*
>
> *Girl Corps Cheered.*
> *The Chippewa Falls girls corps, dressed in their Indian costumes, brought cheers and not a few whistles…But there were other uniforms than the colorful band costume in the files of several of the marching units. The Alonzo Cudworth Sons of the Legion group from Milwaukee had members who wore the uniforms of the United States Army, Navy and Marine men, all of them former service men who had had no opportunity to be fitted for their band uniforms. Judges made allowances for the dress irregularities, and the Cudworth boys won the prize in their division. The Appleton SAL group, which placed second, boasted 17 veterans of World War II.*

Back Stage.
Backstage at the competition was the "back yard" of a circus. Boys and girls, and men and women, waiting to go into competition or resting after their stint, stood around and discussed technicalities of competition, or just tootle on the bugles to warm up their "lip"...

The Winners.
At the massing of the bands, the winners of the competition were announced. With their prizes, they are: River Falls Post No. 121, unopposed winners of the state Class A competition, $350; Meuli-Kilian Unit 77, Legion Auxiliary, of Chippewa Falls, unopposed Auxiliary winners; Cains Post Boy Scout group of Madison, unopposed winners in sponsored group; Curtis O. Reddin Post of Danville, Ill., out-of-state champions, $300; other out-of-state winners were Square Post 232 of Chicago, $250; Gary Memorial Post 232, $200; Peoria Post 2, $150; Melin Romer Post 728 of Chicago, $100, and Charles Roth Post 692 of Oak Park, Ill., $50; Rhinelander and Fond du Lac posts, special exhibition prizes, $50.
—Racine Journal Times, *August 5, 1946*

Happenings in the City
MORE THAN 16,000 persons attended functions at the Horlick Athletic field between last Saturday afternoon and Monday night, according to an estimate by Vic Seitz, field manager. Seitz said 2,200 persons attended the Belle's game Saturday afternoon. 5,400 attended the drum and bugle corps contest Saturday night, 5,889 attended the Belle's game Sunday and 1,947 were at the game Monday night. These do not include participants in the various events nor free admissions.
—Racine Journal Times, *August 5, 1946*

OTHER PERFORMANCES AT HORLICK FIELD BETWEEN 1919 AND 1951

Throughout the period from 1919 to 1951, Racine's drum and bugle corps appeared regularly at Horlick Field at a wide variety of events, most without notice. Here are some of the articles and advertisements that mention drum and bugle corps in Horlick Field.

Racine Belles Semiprofessional Baseball Game

Will Drill Sunday
Roma Lodge drum and bugle corps will give an exhibition drill at Horlick Athletic field Sunday afternoon immediately before the Booster day game between the Racine Belles and the Waukegan Knights. The Roma corps will compete in the music festival in Chicago [Chicagoland Music Festival] *on Saturday and will also appear at the World's fair.*
—Racine Journal Times, *August 16, 1934*

Racine Roma Lodge drum and bugle corps, October 12, 1930. *From left, first row:* Tony Litrenta, Remo Giancinti, Stanley Litrenta, Sam Arnone, Ed Groenke, Carmen DeLuca, Jim Falaschi, Louis DeRose and Guy Policicchio. *Second row:* Ralph Nicotera, Rocco Litrenta, Anthony Litrenta, Peter Vallone, S. Serpe, Michele Sicilia, Joe Arnone and Louis Giacinti. *Third row:* Jerome Litrenta, Frank Marino, John Schiralli, Mike Corona, John Labrasca, Al Constabile, Vincent Cottone, Joe Fillipone and Costraza Vallone. *From the collection of Racine's Roma Lodge.*

Roma Lodge was a leading drum and bugle corps in Racine during the 1930s. It appeared in Horlick Field many times at music festivals and for exhibitions, and it appeared at the Chicagoland Music Festival and the World's Fair, among other events. The unit disbanded around 1940 and sold its uniforms to the Belle City drum and bugle corps, a new Racine drum corps that performed for a short time in the early 1940s. Roma Lodge is an existing fraternal association formed in the 1800s by Racine residents of Italian heritage. You can go to Roma Lodge almost any night for great Italian food.

Softball Game

The Kiltie drum corps will entertain at the game.
—Racine Journal Times, *September 6, 1939*

Rodeo

And, as an added feature will have the Boy Scout drum and bugle corps play on Saturday night before the performance and the Kiltie drum and bugle corps on Sunday.
—Racine Journal Times, *June 18, 1941*

Donkey Baseball Game

The Kiltie drum and bugle corps will perform at Horlick Athletic field between the preliminary and main event.
—Racine Journal Times, *July 3, 1941*

Free Concert

After a winter of intensive rehearsal, the Kiltie Drum and Bugle corps, fully equipped with new drums and bugles, as well as an increased membership, will take the spotlight for 10 minutes in a short drill, its concert number to be directed by the drum major, Bob Thoemke.
—Racine Journal Times, *June 15, 1942*

Navy Relief Benefit Game

Racine Boy Scout Drum Corps To Play Before Navy Ball Game
Racine Boy Scouts drum and bugle corps, one of the finest organizations of its kind in the country, will give a pre-game drill and exhibition when Lieut. Mickey Cochrane's Great Lakes baseball team plays Falk Corporation of Milwaukee in a Navy Relief benefit game at Horlick Athletic field on Tuesday night July 28.
—Racine Journal Times, *June 17, 1942*

Fort Sheridan Athletic Fund Benefit Game

The Kilties drum and bugle corps will entertain at the field at 7:30 o'clock.
—Racine Journal Times, *September 16, 1942*

Racine Belles Game

Featured, too, will be the Racine Boy Scout drum and bugle corps, fresh from its triumph in competition at Kenosha Sunday night.
—Racine Journal Times, *August 24, 1943*

Racine Belles Double-header

The Racine Post 76 American Legion drum and bugle corps will entertain with concert numbers between games.
—Racine Journal Times, *August 31, 1943*

Racine Belles Game

August 11, 1944.

Racine Belles' Last Game of the Season

And the Boy Scout drum and bugle corps also performed.
—Racine Journal Times, *September 7, 1944*

War Benefit Baseball Game Advertisement

The Racine Boy Scouts Drum & Bugle Corps Will Play at 7:30.
—*June 7, 1945*

Racine Belles Game

August 15, 1945.

American Legion vs. VFW Baseball Game

July 2, 1946.

Moose Major Fastpitch League Game

Moose Major Fastpitch league team will play the Eagles Tuesday night at 8 p.m. at Horlick Athletic Field. Preceding the game at 7:30 p.m. the Kiltie Drum & Bugle Corps will play.
—Racine Journal Times, *August 30, 1946*

FAST PITCH SOFTBALL
MOOSE LODGE 437 vs. F. O. E. AERIE 281
HORLICK ATHLETIC FIELD, RACINE
Game Time 8:00 p. m.
TUESDAY, SEPT. 3, 1946
RECEIPTS TO MOOSE AND EAGLES VETS
Admission 50c
Tax 10c
TOTAL 60c
KILTIE DRUM AND BUGLE CORPS for Added Attraction
Beginning at 7:30
ENTERTAINMENT GALORE

September 3, 1946.

Semiprofessional Football Game

Legion Drum Corps To Perform Sunday
Racine's American Legion Drum and Bugle Corps will perform Sunday afternoon between the halves of the Legion-Whiting, Indiana, semi-pro football game at Horlick Athletic Field. The 64 piece corps directed by Wilbur Hansen, is one of the outstanding musical organizations in the American Legion. It has won four consecutive first place awards in national Legion convention competition. Sunday afternoon the corps will perform the drills which have brought it national fame.
—Racine Journal Times, *October 17, 1947*

Racine Belles Home Opener

May 11, 1948.

Racine Belles Game

> *DRUMMING UP A WINNER? Police Chief Wilbur Hansen, who doubles as drum major of Legion Post 76 drum and bugle corps, and Louis Niesen watch as the Racine Belles fleet outfielder, Edie Perlick, drums up a possible double victory for Racine. The drum corps, four times national champions, will seek another title at the National American Legion convention in Miami in October. The Racine Belles, girls, world baseball champions twice, seek a third crown. Racine residents will be able to see both in action Monday night (Labor Day) at Horlick Athletic Field. The Belles play a double header with Rockford and between games the Legion corps will put on its final full dress exhibition drill prior to convention appearance.*
> —*caption from the* Racine Journal Times, *September 2, 1948*

The Rockford team, the Peaches, was the team featured in the movie *A League of Their Own*. The final game of the movie is between the Peaches and the Belles.

Racine Bees Semiprofessional Football Game Advertisement

> *Legion Corps to Play—As an added attraction, the Legion Drum and Bugle Corps will put on a full dress rehearsal at halftime. This will be the corps' final Racine appearance before the National Legion parade in Miami.*
> —*October 2, 1948*

Racine Bees Semiprofessional Football Game Advertisements

The Legion, Kilties and Scouts appeared at three consecutive Racine Bees semipro football games: Legion on October 3, Kilties on October 13 and the Scouts on October 20. The Bees ran ads for each game in which the only significant changes were the opponent, the date and time and the drum and bugle corps.

National Fastball League Double-header

> *Boy Scouts Drum and Bugle Corps will entertain between games.*
> —Racine Journal Times, *August 5, 1949*

October 3, 1948.

Racine Belles Game

Sunday night will be American Legion Night in Racine with Post 310 sponsoring the sale of tickets and Post 76's state champion drum and bugle corps staging a 15-minute pre-game exhibition.
—Racine Journal Times, *August 26, 1949*

Racine Belles Game

Racine Boy Scouts drum and bugle corps will give a 15-minute performance starting at 7:45.
—Racine Journal Times, *September 2, 1949*

Racine Belles Opening Day Game

May 18, 1950.

National Fastball League Double-header

American Legion Post 76 state champion drum and bugle corps will demonstrate its championship performance between games of this latter doubleheader.
—Racine Journal Times, *August 19, 1950*

National Fastball League Double-header

American Legion Post 76 drum and bugle corps will give an exhibition performance between games.
—Racine Journal Times, *July 18, 1951*

Wisconsin-Illinois Fastball League Game

Interspersed with the sports features will be...a performance by the Armenian Youth drum and bugle corps.
—Racine Journal Times, *August 16, 1951*

Chapter 2

Horlick Field Develops A Reputation

1952–1961

In 1952, Horlick Athletic Field began hosting annual drum and bugle corps shows. From 1952 to 1961, Horlick Athletic Field hosted an average of one show a year. Units that regularly appeared included Chicago Cavaliers, Madison Boy Scouts, Norwood Park Legion/Imperials, Mercury Thunderbolts and Americanos. Senior corps that appeared included Skokie Indians, Edison Lamplighters, Spirit of St. Louis, Hamm's Indians, Canada's Marching Ambassadors and the famous Commonwealth Edison of Chicago.

During this ten-year period, Horlick Field's reputation grew. Word spread of the knowledgeable, appreciative audience; professionally run and reliable show organizations; good prize money; and always-tough competition.

1952

Horlick Athletic Field hosted two drum and bugle corps shows in 1952, and they were the models for all the shows that it would host for decades. Performances by historic champions and current contenders, thousands in the stands and ten drum and bugle corps per show were the standards throughout Horlick Field's long history of hosting shows.

June 1, 1952—Racine Boy Scouts Twenty-fifth Anniversary Show

Scouts Pay for Own Party
When the Racine Boy Scout Drum & Bugle Corps decided to celebrate its twenty-fifth anniversary, the Scouts did not ask the community to hold a birthday party for them. They planned the party themselves and as many Racine people as can get into Horlick Athletic Field Sunday afternoon will be the Scouts' non-paying guests at a fine musical show and drum corps exhibition. Ten corps, including the Scouts, the American Legion, Kiltie and Armenian Corps from Racine, and six out-of-town units will play and march.

No one but the boys in the Scout corps is footing the bill for this party. No solicitations have been made, no hand-outs asked, no tickets sold, and no "program" packed with advertising has been sold. The Scouts raised the money through paper collection drives, doing odd jobs, and dues. The event will cost the Scouts about $700, and their Mother's Club will spend $300 to $400 feeding visiting corps…These boys have carried Racine's name from one end of America to the other, and have been honored as the finest Scout drum corps in the nation. Sunday afternoon they will take the opportunity to say "thank you" to their home town, in its support and encouragement.
—Racine Journal Times, *May 27, 1952*

The Racine Boy Scouts Twenty-fifth Anniversary show was a free show given by the Scouts to the people of Racine for the support that Racine had given the corps over the years. It was a very good show. Four of the eleven corps in this show were national championship finalists. General George Bell of Chicago would likely have been a fifth finalist, but the corps didn't go to the 1952 championship in Los Angeles. General Bell had taken second in 1950 and fifth in 1951 at the VFW championships.

June 1, 1952—Racine Boy Scouts Twenty-fifth Anniversary Show
All Exhibition
Madison Scouts
Racine Legion (Boys of '76)..A10
General George Bell

RONNIE PERKINS
Tenor Drummer

You're Invited

TO THE BOY SCOUT DRUM AND BUGLE CORPS 25th BIRTHDAY PARTY

SUNDAY, JUNE 1st

HORLICK FIELD

2:00 P. M.

This program is our treat, it is our way of saying "Thank you" to the people of Racine who have been our friends and boosters for twenty-five years.

We consider it a great privilege to represent Scouting and the City of Racine and thru this Silver Anniversary Program we are expressing our thanks for your help.

The Racine Scout Corps

COME OUT AND BE OUR GUESTS AT THE BIGGEST DRUM CORPS COMPETITION EVER HELD IN RACINE

The Following Corps Will Participate

Boys of '76, Racine American Legion
Racine Kilties
Armenian Youth Federation of Racine
Evanston Lancers, Evanston Elks Club
General George Bell Corps, V.F.W., Chicago
Madison Scouts, Madison, Wis.
Norwood Park, Ill., Legion Corps
Austin Grenadiers of Chicago
Mercy High School All Girls Corps, Milwaukee
The Racine Scout Corps
Mel Tierney Corps of Park Ridge, Ill. (Formerly Logan Square)

Everyone is Invited . . .

TO COME OUT AND ENJOY AN AFTERNOON OF FUN AND MUSIC

No Admission Charge . . . This Is On Us!!!

Above: The Racine Scouts, Horlick Field, June 6, 1952. *Racine Heritage Museum.*

Opposite, top: The Chicago-area Norwood Park Imperials, Horlick Field, June 6, 1952. Norwood appeared in Horlick Field thirteen times. *Racine Heritage Museum.*

Opposite, bottom: Our Lady of Mercy High School drum and bugle corps, Horlick Field, June 6, 1952. *Racine Heritage Museum.*

Mel Tierney (Skokie Vanguard) A3
Kilties
Racine Scouts
Norwood Park Legion (Imperials) A11
Austin Grenadiers A12
Armenian Youth Federation
Evanston Lancers
Mercy High School All-girl

NORWOOD PARK
POST
740
CHICAGO

MERCY HIGH SCHOOL
MILWAUKEE

TONIGHT
7:30 P. M. at HORLICK FIELD
Giant MIDWEST
Drum Corps
CONTEST
SEE THE FINEST MIDWEST DRUM CORPS IN ACTION
Featuring . . .
★ PORT WASHINGTON, WIS. ★ SKOKIE, ILL.
★ COMMONWEALTH EDISON ★ LaPORTE, IND.
★ SHARVIN RED JACKETS ★ RACINE KILTIES
★ RACINE LEGION ★ GROSS YAKISH DRILL TEAM
Admission – Inc. Tax – ADULTS $1.00, CHILDREN $.50
AMERICAN LEGION US
• Sponsored by •
Racine Post "76" Drum Corps

JULY 5, 1952—GIANT MIDWEST DRUM CORPS CONTEST

Drum Corps to Compete In Goodwill Celebration
Six nationally noted drum corps, including former national champions, will compete at Horlick Athletic Field in Racine Saturday, July 5, as a feature of the three day Goodwill celebration. The six belong to a "Midwest Legion Drum Corps League," in which units from each city compete in each city during the summer months. They include La Porte, Ind., Commonwealth Edison of Chicago, Sharvin Post of Chicago, Skokie of Chicago, Port Washington and Racine Legion.
—Racine Journal Times, *June 18, 1952*

The Boys of '76's first annual show was a very good show with seven corps and three championship finalist units. It was the only Horlick Field appearance of Commonwealth Edison from Chicago, an annual powerhouse at American Legion nationals. Commonwealth made all but one American Legion national finals contest from 1934 through 1958. It took first in 1936, 1940 and 1941; second in 1934, 1938, 1946, 1950 and 1956; third in 1935; fourth in 1947 and 1949; fifth in 1948; sixth in 1951; seventh in 1937 and 1958; eighth in 1955; tenth in 1952, 1954 and 1957; and twelfth in 1953. And it took fourth in this show. Commonwealth did not go to American Legion nationals in 1959 and folded in 1960.

The Boys of '76 hosted its annual drum and bugle corps show as part of Racine's traditional and long Fourth of July celebration, called the Goodwill Celebration. After a few years, this annual Fourth of July–timed show became known as the Goodwill Spectacular.

JULY 5, 1952—GIANT MIDWEST DRUM CORPS CONTEST

1. 90.7 Skokie Indians..A7
2. 89.1 Port Washington Legion
3. 88.6 La Porte Lancers
4. 86.6 Commonwealth Edison....................................A10
5. Sharvin Red Jackets

Exhibition

Kilties
Boys of '76 (Racine Legion)..A9

Meanwhile, at Horlick Athletic Field Saturday night, the first Tri-State Midwest Drum and Bugle Corps contest was held before about 1,000 persons. The Skokie (Ill.) American Legion Drum and Bugle Corps copped first place honors, with Port Washington (Wis.) American Legion Drum and Bugle Corps taking second. Third place honors went to the Legion Drum and bugle Corps of La Porte, Ind. And the largest unit, from Chicago, the Commonwealth Edison Corps, drew fourth place.

Kilties Give Exhibition
Post 76 Drum and Bugle Corps of Racine participated, but because it was host, did not compete. The Racine YMCA Kilties gave an exhibition. The Gross-Yakisk Drill Team of Milwaukee, VFW national champions in 1951, also put on an exhibition. Judges in the contest were all members of the Midwest Drum and Bugle Corps Association.
—Racine Journal Times, *July 7, 1952*

Chicagoans Appreciate Goodwill Celebration
Dear Tex: For several years it has been our privilege to spend the Fourth of July in Racine and we'd like you to know we think this year's celebration the finest we've seen. Beginning with the parade, which was beautiful, and ending with the Legion's Drum & Bugle Corps competitive program, we enjoyed entertainment second to none. To the committee who so well planned this fine fair and to the civic-minded citizens who sponsored it, through your column we'd like to say—Congratulations!
Mr. and Mrs. George Olson.
Chicago, Ill.
—Racine Journal Times, *July 14, 1952*

July 5, 1953—Giant Midwest Drum Corps Contest

Legion Drum Corps Enters Contest in Racine on July 5
The Racine American Legion Drum and Bugle Corps will face competition from champion Legion drum corps of two Midwestern states in the drum and bugle corps contest at Horlick Field July 5. The YMCA Kilties and the Racine Boy Scouts drum corps will give exhibitions at the contest which will start at 7:30 p.m. Sunday, July 5.

Featured as a part of the July 4th Goodwill Celebration, the drum corps competition, sponsored by the Racine Legion Drum and Bugle Corps last year was won by the Skokie, Ill., Drum and Bugle Corps. This unit will return this year. It has won the Illinois state Legion championship and placed seventh at the American Legion national convention.

Other out-of-state corps competing will be the Sharvin Red Jackets of the North Chicago American Legion, former Illinois Legion champions, and the Hamon Gray Post 83 Drum and Bugle Corps of La Porte, Ind. The unit is the present Indiana state Legion Champ and has held this title 20 times in the past. Wisconsin's Class B champions in Legion competition for many years, the Port Washington Drum and Bugle Corps, will compete this year in Racine in Class A competition.

—Racine Journal Times, *June 25, 1953*

The 1953 contest was the first of only three shows to be scheduled at Horlick Field that were rained out. A standstill was held a few blocks away at William Horlick High School gymnasium.

June 26, 1954—VFW State Championship

Four Enter Competition

John Stolberg, convention parade chairman, has announced that four mid-west drum and bugle corps will be entered in the open competition scheduled for 8 p.m. June 26 at Horlick Field. They are the Grenadiers from American Legion Post 597, Chicago, the Four Lakes Boys Scouts Drum and Bugle Corps of Madison, The Gladiators of VFW Woodrow Wilson Post 11, Milwaukee, and the Norwood Park Drum and Bugle Corps of the Capt. Wm. J. Clark VFW Post 3627 of Chicago, Ill.

Two drum corps will appear in the VFW drum corps competition, limited to organizations in which 60 per cent or more of the organization are VFW members. They are the Wolf Olson VFW Post 1230 Drum and Bugle Corps of Sheboygan, and the Thomas Rooney VFW Post 1530 Drum and Bugle Corps of La Crosse. The sole entrant in the women's drum and bugle corps competition is the Henry J. Schaefer VFW Post 2925 unit of Milwaukee.

These units will be joined by the Racine American Legion Drum Corps, the Boy Scouts Drum and Bugle Corps, the YMCA Kilties Drum and

> *Bugle Corps, the Armenian Youth Drum and Bugle Corps, The Racine Elks All-City Youth Band and S.C. Johnson & Son, Inc. band in the parade. Most of the units will also give exhibition during the competition Saturday night.*
>
> —Racine Journal Times, *June 14, 1954*

The 1954 VFW State Championship contest included the junior drum corps that took second at VFW and seventh and eighth at American Legion and the twelfth-place American Legion senior corps. It had eleven corps, four of them championship finalists, and one senior all-female drum corps.

The Elks Youth Band made its first appearance at a Horlick Field drum and bugle corps event. It would be in exhibition at most drum and bugle corps shows in Horlick Field for the next thirty years. It was a band that looked and performed like a drum corps; it just had woodwinds. It won VFW nationals many times over the years. At the 1964 and 1968 VFW national contests, the Racine Kilties won the VFW drum and bugle corps title and the Racine Elks won the VFW band title.

JUNE 26, 1954—VFW STATE CHAMPIONSHIP

Juniors

1. 90.8 Austin Grenadiers A7
2. 90.6 Madison Scouts V2
3. 88.8 Norwood Park Imperials
4. 88.6 Gladiators

Seniors

1. Wolf-Olson VFW Post 1230, Sheboygan
2. Thomas Rooney VFW Post 1530, La Crosse

Auxiliary

1. Henry J. Schaefer VFW Post 2925, Milwaukee (Schaefer Ladies)

Exhibition

Racine Scouts
Kilties A8
Boys of '76 .... A12
Armenian Youth

JULY 2, 1955—FOURTH ANNUAL MIDWEST DRUM CORPS CONTEST

The Fourth Annual Midwest Drum Corps Contest was another good show with the second-place VFW unit and the fifth- and seventh-place American Legion units.

The Cavaliers made its first appearance in Horlick Field at this show. It took fifth at American Legion championships in 1955. The corps did not enter VFW nationals competition until 1956, when it took first in prelims by a point over perennial champion St. Vincent's Cadets.

The 1955 contest hosted the second and last appearance in Horlick Field by the Evanston Lancers. The third-place Mercury Thunderbolts from Cedarburg, Wisconsin, was a competitive unit that often beat corps such as the Kilties, Racine Scouts and Norwood Park Imperials in the 1950s.

Read This Twice!!
POST 76 AMERICAN LEGION
DRUM & BUGLE CORPS
Presents FLASH and CLASS
The 4th Annual
Midwest
DRUM CORPS CONTEST
Horlick Athletic Field
Sat., July 2 - 7:30 P.M.
6 of the leading Midwestern Drum Corps!
See our local corps competitors in action!
• Chicago Cavaliers
• Evanston Lancers
• Madison Scouts
• Norwood Park Imperials
• Mercury Thunderbolts
• Racine Kilties
• Intermission exhibition by Racine Elks Youth Band. Also Racine Misfits Original Drill.
Admission Adults $1.00, Children 50c

July 2, 1955—Fourth Annual Midwest Drum Corps Contest

1. 87.9 Madison Scouts..V2
2. 86.4 Cavaliers..A5
3. 84.7 Mercury Thunderbolts
4. 82.9 Norwood Park Imperials....................................A7
5. 79.7 Evanston Lancers

Exhibition

Kilties

Boys of '76

July 3, 1956—Fifth Annual Midwest Drum Corps Contest

The Cavaliers appeared for the second straight year and would appear a total of six times between 1955 and 1964. While the show had only six drum and bugle corps and the Racine Elks Youth Band, it had the Cavaliers, which took third at VFW, and Boys of '76, which took fifth at American Legion.

July 3, 1956—Fifth Annual Midwest Drum Corps Contest

1. 87.1 Cavaliers..V3
2. 84.1 Militaires
3. 83.4 Racine Scouts
4. 82.8 Kilties
5. 80.0 Mercury Thunderbolts

Exhibition

Boys of '76 ....A5

July 3, 1957—Seventh Annual Midwest Drum Corps Contest

For some reason, Boys of '76 skipped a year and went from the Fifth Annual Contest to the Seventh Annual Contest. This show is notable because it has drum and bugle corps only from Wisconsin. Of the ninety-nine drum and bugle corps shows held in Horlick Field, this is the only Class A contest—other than VFW and American Legion state contests—that did not have an out-of-state drum corps. Three Class B/C shows also had only Wisconsin units.

The Appleton, Wisconsin Americanos, a competitive and entertaining Wisconsin drum corps formed in 1936, first appeared in Horlick Field in 1946. Throughout its history, it had a Spanish theme and red and black colors. The Militaires was formed in 1956 and merged with the Milwaukee Starlites in the 1960s. Drum Corps Hall of Fame member Dave Richards got his start in drum corps as a member of the Militaires. The Militaires took second behind the Cavaliers in 1956 and second behind Madison Scouts in 1957. The Militaires beat the hometown Kilties and Racine Scouts in both contests.

July 3, 1957—Seventh Annual Midwest Drum Corps Contest

1. 89.7 Madison Scouts..V5 A2
2. 85.1 Militaires
3. 81.8 Racine Scouts
4. 79.7 Kilties
5. 77.9 Mercury Thunderbolts
6. 77.8 Americanos

Exhibition

Boys of '76

July 3, 1958—Midwest Drum and Bugle Corps Contest

Championship drum corps, bands and drill teams will share top billing with jazz in Thursday's Goodwill celebration events. The night of music will feature the precision skills of marching units at the outdoor Midwest Drum and Bugle Corps competition, starting at 7:30 p.m. in Horlick Athletic Field. Lineup of the drum corps for the Horlick Field competition includes the Madison Boy Scouts, two-time winners of the Wisconsin Spectacle of Music, national open class champions of 1954 and winners of the statewide Veterans of Foreign Wars competition last year and national champions the year before. Also in the lineup from out-of-town will be the Mercury Thunderbolts of Cedarburg, Wis., first place winners in state competition. Other of the visiting corps will be the Appleton, Wis. Americanos and the Norwood Park, Ill. Imperials.

New Kiltie Uniform
Competing also will be the Racine Boy Scout Drum and Bugle Corps and the YMCA Kilties Drum and Bugle Corps. The Kilties will present for the first time a new uniform, made of McAndrews plaid imported from Scotland. The tartan is of powder blue and red, with the blue the predominant color, replacing the traditional red jackets and yellow and black plaid which the corps has worn in the past.

In addition to the six competing corps the four-hour show will feature exhibitions one by the Racine Elks' Youth Band which leaves Friday for its New York City tour and appearances at the national Elks convention. In exhibition will also be the Racine American Legion "Boys of '76" sponsors of the competition.

Thursday's competition will come under the experienced and expert eye of the All-American Drum Corps Judges' Assn., an exacting group of men, trained to ferret out the slightest deviation from perfection.
—Racine Journal Times, *July 2, 1958*

2 Drum Corps in New Garb
Racine's Boy Scout Drum and Bugle Corps, along with the YMCA Kilties, will step out in new uniforms at tonight's Midwest Drum Corps competition in Horlick Athletic Field. The scouts will wear official olive drab, wool gabardine uniforms with white neckerchiefs and the corps emblem. The smoother gabardine replaces the wool serge uniform. The Kilties will introduce a powder blue tartan, replacing the traditional yellow and black plaid with red jackets.
—Racine Journal Times, *July 3, 1958*

No ads could be found for this show. The show is called the Midwest Drum and Bugle Corps Contest, without mentioning an annual number, in the newspaper article below.

Madison Scouts appeared for the fifth time in seven years and won the third straight Horlick Field contest in which it appeared. Overall, Madison won twelve Horlick Field contests, tied with the Kilties for most wins in Horlick Field. The show had seven corps, three of which were championship finalists.

JULY 3, 1958—MIDWEST DRUM AND BUGLE CORPS CONTEST

1. 89.3 Madison Scouts..V5 A6
2. 86.2 Norwood Park Imperials..............................V7
3. 82.1 Kilties...A11
4. 78.9 Mercury Thunderbolts
5. 77.4 Racine Scouts
6. 76.8 Americanos

Exhibition

Boys of '76

> *Madison Wins Midwest Title*
>
> *Martial music and jazz were the musical themes for two events staged Thursday evening as part of Racine's 22d Goodwill Celebration. Top honors at the Midwest Drum and Bugle Corps competition before 2,500 spectators at Horlick Athletic Field were won by the Madison Boy Scouts. The unit was also the first to receive the Thomas O. Penn Memorial Traveling trophy, provided by the family of the former member of the Racine American Legion Boys of '76 Drum and Bugle Corps, which sponsored the competition.*
>
> *The Norwood Park, Ill., Imperials were second in the drum corps competition and the Racine Kilties third. Fourth place in the event judged by All-American Drum Corps Judges' Assn. members went to the Mercury Thunderbolts of Cedarburg, Wis. The Racine Boy Scouts were fifth and the Appleton, Wis., Americanos placed sixth. Cash prizes for the winning organizations ranged from $100 to $250.*
>
> —Racine Journal Times, *July 5, 1958*

The rare picture below shows the Mercury Thunderbolts in competition in Horlick Field on July 5, 1958. It also shows the football field layout that existed from 1925 through 1963. The view faces south to the outfield bleachers from the baseball infield. The Thunderbolts appears to have twenty-four horns and flags only in the American flag section. Corps began to have larger flag lines that moved with the horns during the late 1950s. In 1968, just ten years later, the Des Plaines Vanguard had thirty-four flags.

Cedarburg Mercury Thunderbolts in Horlick Field, 1958. *From the collection of John Schoenknecht.*

Cedarburg Mercury Thunderbolts, 1958. The inspection judge is Midwest icon Chris Prentice. *From the collection of John Schoenknecht.*

A DIGRESSION: HORLICK FIELD AND BEER

THEN THERE'S a bit of criticism connected with the Drum Corps Show held at Horlick Athletic Field Thursday night. A prominent industrial leader says:
"You couldn't buy pop in the stands. If you wanted some, you had to go down to a refreshment booth to get it. But hawkers of beer were all over the place, stepping on your feet, getting in your way and in at least some cases, probably selling beer to youngsters not old enough to buy it in a tavern. I don't object to people drinking beer. But on an occasion like that, when there's a fine crowd that wants to see the corps in action and listen to the music, I think the beer hawkers should have been barred. Especially since it was a civic event held in a public park."
—Racine Journal Times, *July 5, 1958*

When talking to drum and bugle corps veterans about their visit to Horlick Field, the phrase "and they sold beer!" was often heard, as if that were shocking. All spoke with delight about it though, and many added that they hoisted a few themselves. Those of us from Wisconsin find this amusing. It is Wisconsin. Beer is never far away.

The letter to the editor above attests to the fact that beer was once sold not only at the concession stand at Horlick Field but also by vendors in the stands themselves.

You can go to a Racine Raiders semiprofessional football game in Horlick Field any fall and hoist a cold one in remembrance of how good the last one tasted at one of those hot, muggy Horlick Athletic Field drum and bugle corps shows.

JULY 3, 1959—EIGHTH ANNUAL GOODWILL DRUM AND BUGLE CORPS CONTEST

The Horlick Field audience was by this time familiar with and expected the best that the country had to offer. Madison Scouts had already appeared as a second-place national contest finalist in three different years. But 1959 was the first year that Horlick Field hosted the national championship drum and bugle corps, something it would do twenty-one times between 1959 and 2008.

Boys of '76 got back on track with the annual number in its ads this year.

July 3, 1959—Eighth Annual Goodwill Drum and Bugle Corps Contest

1. 87.4 Cavaliers..V1 A2
2. 79.1 Norwood Park Imperials........................A6
3. 75.0 Kilties..A9
4. 71.6 Americanos
5. 69.9 Racine Scouts
6. 63.0 Mercury Thunderbolts

Exhibition

Boys of '76 ....A7
Racine Junior Scouts

July 3, 1960—Goodwill Spectacular

6 Senior Corps Enter Contest
A Midwest "preview" of the national American Legion convention's drum and bugle corps contest will be held at Horlick Field July 3 as part of the Goodwill Fourth of July celebration. The event, sponsored by the "Boys of '76" American Legion corps will feature an all-senior competition between half a dozen midwestern state champions…First place winner will receive $800 of the total $3,300 prize money. Scheduled to compete are: Skokie "Indians." Illinois Legion champion and former national champion; Kewanee, Ill., "Black Knights"; Michigan Legion champion Detroit "Lamplighters"; Ohio Legion Champion Bellefontaine "Angels"; Missouri Legion champion St. Louis "Spirit of St. Louis"; and the Indiana Legion champion La Porte "Lancers"…The Pittsburgh "Rockets," holders of the Pennsylvania Legion senior corps title, have been invited but final arrangements haven't been completed. Racine's Legion Corps, Wisconsin Legion champion, will perform an exhibition.
—Racine Journal Times, *June 13, 1960*

The 1960 Spectacular, billed as a Senior Invitational, had five of the top ten senior units at the 1960 American Legion senior championships, including the third-place American Legion finalist Skokie Indians and second-place VFW finalist Edison Lamplighters. It also had the Kilties, which took ninth at VFW Nationals. In all, the show had eight drum corps with six championship finalist units. There were five thousand in attendance.

Skokie Indians and Kewanee Black Knights had been senior powers for years. Spirit of St. Louis, based about four hundred miles away, appeared in Horlick Field seven times between 1960 and 1966. The Edison Lamplighters from Detroit, formed in 1932, placed second at VFW nationals in both 1959 and 1960.

Boys of '76's annual Fourth of July show had been associated with Racine's Fourth of July Goodwill Celebration from the start. In 1960, it became an official activity of the celebration and took on the name the Goodwill Spectacular, the name it would bear through the era of great contests.

July 3, 1960—Goodwill Spectacular

1. 66.000 Skokie Indians A3
2. 64.200 Bellefontaine Angels
3. 63.600 Edison Lamplighters A9 V2
4. 59.975 Spirit of St. Louis A10
5. 58.200 Kewanee Black Knights A7

Exhibition

Racine Scouts

Kilties V9

(69.475) Boys of '76 .... A6

July 1, 1961—Twelfth Annual Goodwill Spectacular

It's clear that Boys of '76 was unclear on the number of shows that it had hosted. If the 1959 show was the Eighth Annual Show, as it said in its ads, then this should have been the Tenth Annual. This is an example of the ad hoc, volunteer and often chaotic operations of most drum and bugle corps of the time.

The 1961 show was also billed as a Senior Invitational and had three of the top five units at the 1961 American Legion senior championships and the Kilties, which took eleventh at VFW nationals. Of the nine corps in the show, four were championship finalist units.

Canada's Marching Ambassadors had its beginnings in 1926 in a military trumpet and bugle band of the Canadian army. In 1959, members of the band joined together to start the Marching Ambassadors drum and bugle corps as an activity outside the military. The Marching Ambassadors' military precision and skills delighted audiences in Canada and the United States for years. In this show, the Canadian unit easily defeated the drum corps that finished fourth and fifth at American Legion nationals in 1959. In both the 1960 and 1961 contests, Boys of '76, in judged exhibition, would have won the show by several points. This gives an indication of how good Boys of '76 was at the time. It took second at American Legion in 1961.

JULY 1, 1961—TWELFTH ANNUAL GOODWILL SPECTACULAR

1. 71.25 Marching Ambassadors
2. 65.00 Spirit of St. Louis..A5
3. 62.40 Edison Lamplighters
4. 59.95 Kewanee Black Knights A4
5. 42.05 Kenosha Kingsmen

Exhibition

(75.20) Boys of '76 ....A2
(65.45) Kilties V11
(62.47) Racine Scouts

—Journal-Times Photo

Drum majors of the corps competing Saturday night at Horlick Athletic Field are, from left, John Brintnall of the Kenosha Kingsmen; Robert Carruthers of the Marching Ambassadors of Toronto, Can.; Willie Bates of the St. Louis unit, "Spirit of St. Louis;" Robert Cunningham of the Kewaunee, Ill., Black Knights, and William Hock of the Detroit Lamplighters. Four of the corps ranked among the top 10 in the last National American Legion competion.

Canadian Unit Is Top Corps

A capacity crowd at Horlick Athletic Field Saturday night watched the Marching Ambassadors of Toronto, Can., win the American Legion Post 76 sponsored drum corps competition.

The Canadian corps, making its first appearance in the Racine event, scored 71.25 points. Scores of the other four competing corps, in order, were Spirit of St. Louis, 65; Detroit Lamplighters, 62.40; Kewaunee, Ill., Black Knights, 59.95, and the Kenosha Kingsmen, 42.05.

Three of Racine's drum corps, judged on the same basis as the visiting corps during their exhibition performances, all scored above the third rated in the competition. The American Legion Boys of 76 topped the scoring with 75.20; YMCA Kilties earned a 65.45 and the Racine Boy Scouts scored 62.47.

Post-show article and picture from the *Racine Journal Times*, July 2, 1961.

OTHER PERFORMANCES AT HORLICK FIELD BETWEEN 1952 AND 1961

Even as Horlick Field was developing a reputation for holding quality drum corps shows, Racine's drum and bugle corps continued to serve Horlick Field in its traditional way: providing musical entertainment at outdoor events.

Racine Raiders Semiprofessional Football Game Advertisement

Legion drum & Bugle Corps Will Entertain Between Games
—August 8, 1952

Racine Raiders Semiprofessional Football Game Advertisement

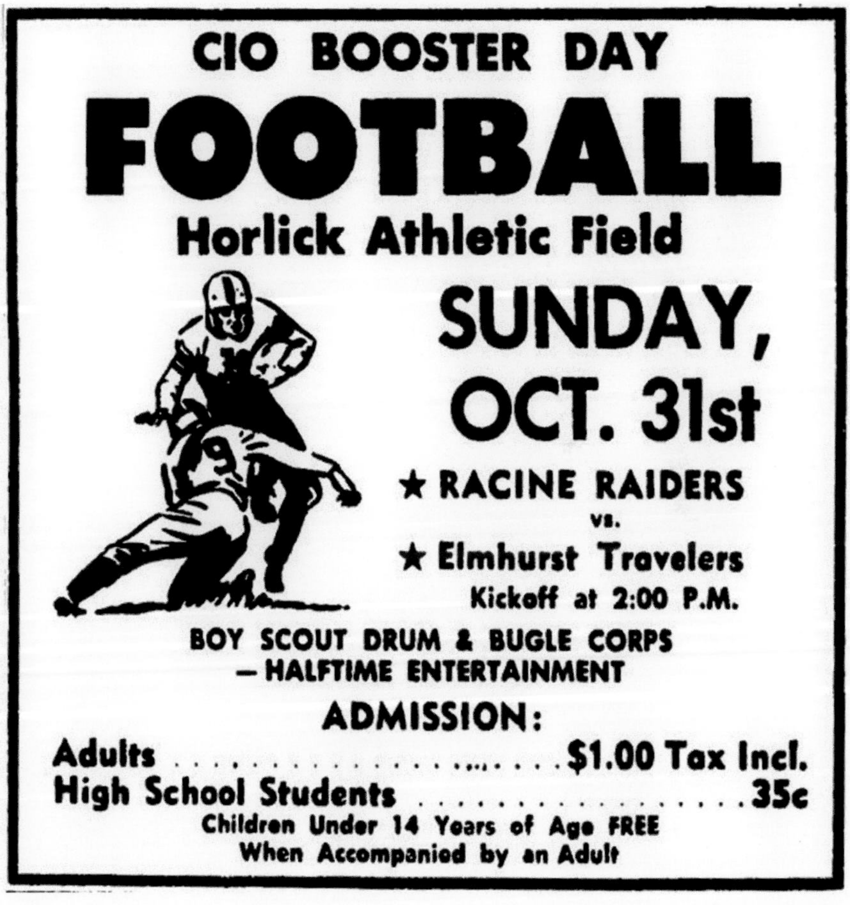

October 30, 1954.

Racine Raiders Semiprofessional Football Game

American Legion Post 76 drum and bugle corps will present an exhibition between halves of the Raider-Delavan game.
—Racine Journal Times, *October 14, 1956*

Tri-State League Fastball Game

The boy scout drum and bugle corps will perform starting at 7 tomorrow night.
—Racine Journal Times, *May 24, 1957*

Southeast District Semipro Tournament Baseball Game Advertisement

Legion Drum Corps Exhibition 8 P.M.
—August 3, 1957

Chapter 3

THE GOLDEN YEARS

1962–1978

Horlick Athletic Field was a phenomenon in the seventeen years between 1962 and 1978. In these years, Horlick Field hosted:

- Fifty-seven drum and bugle corps shows, an average of almost three and a half shows a year
- Over 541* individual drum and bugle corps performances, an average of almost 10 performances per show and 32 performances per year
- The VFW/DCI/DCA/American Legion champion nineteen times—an average of more than once in every three shows and once a year
- The top four VFW/DCI corps in one show twice
- The top three VFW/DCI corps in one show five times
- Seven championship finalist drum corps in one show four times
- Six championship finalist drum corps in one show seven times
- 158 performances of a championship finalist from that same year, an average of 9 finalist performances per year

*The drum and bugle corps at one show are unknown, and many exhibition corps that appeared were not recorded.

In show after show, the Racine audience kept filling the Horlick Field grandstands to capacity and cheering on the corps to unparalleled emotional performances. It began in spectacular fashion at the Goodwill Spectacular on July 3, 1962, with a nine-corps, seven-finalist show that included the VFW's top two drum and bugle corps of 1962.

Chapter 4

THE LEGEND BEGINS

1962

1962 STATISTICS

Shows	3
Drum corps performances	30
States represented	8
VFW champion performances	1
Championship finalist performances	14

The year 1962 set the stage for Horlick Field for the next seventeen years: it had three shows, corps from several states, top-tier drum and bugle corps and thousands in the stands for each show. There were two junior shows and a senior association championship show.

JULY 3—GOODWILL SPECTACULAR

After hosting arguably the two best Midwest senior drum and bugle corps contests in 1960 and 1961, in 1962, the Goodwill Spectacular returned to junior corps competition. The July 3 show—as it was known in Racine even when the show happened to occur on a different date—was the first time that a Horlick Field show hosted the first- and second-place corps at VFW nationals in one show, something it would do for three straight years and a total of eight times between 1962 and 1978. This was also the first time

"GOODWILL SPECTACULAR"
Jr. Drum and Bugle Corps Contest
Sponsored by
American Legion
"BOYS OF '76"
DRUM & BUGLE CORPS
TUES. JULY 3
7:30 P.M.
Horlick Field
Adults $1.50 Children Under 12 75c
AMERICAN LEGION
U.S.
In Competition:
• CHICAGO ROYAL AIRS • MADISON SCOUTS
(Royal Airs Finished 2nd in 1961 National American Legion Junior Competition
• NORWOOD PARK IMPERIALS
• RACINE SCOUTS • RACINE KILTIES
• CHICAGO CAVALIERS
Exhibitions by:
Kiltie Kadets — "Boys of '76" —
(Boys of '76 Finished 2nd in 1961 National American Legion Senior Competition)
Racine Jr. Boy Scouts — Racine Elks Youth Band

The 1962 Goodwill Spectacular Program cover page. *Racine Heritage Museum.*

that Horlick Field hosted seven finalists in one show. All six corps in this competition made finals at VFW nationals in 1962, and the host Boys of '76 finished second at the senior American Legion nationals.

This was the first of only five appearances in Horlick Field by the Chicago Royal Airs. Sadly for the fans in Racine, the Royal Airs did not appear in Horlick Field in 1965.

July 3, 1962—Goodwill Spectacular

1. 83.100 Cavaliers..V1
2. 82.525 Royal Airs..V2 A2
3. 79.550 Madison Scouts...V6
4. 76.600 Norwood Park Imperials..............................V7
5. 75.625 Racine Scouts...V12
6. 74.950 Kilties...V11

Exhibition

Boys of '76 ....A2
Racine Junior Scouts
Kiltie Kadets

ROYAL AIRS Cicero, Illinois

The Royal Airs of Cicero, Illinois, are sponsored by Cicero Post # 96 of the American Legion, and Patrick T. Hallinan Post # 3580, Blue Island, Ill., Veterans of Foreign Wars.

The corps was formed in June of 1958, on the grass of a public park, and entered competition.

In 1960 they placed first in the Winter Carnival contest at St. Paul, Minn., first in the Madison Heights, Michigan, V.F.W. contest and fifth in the American Legion National contest at Miami, Florida.

The season of 1961 was a very successful season for the Royal Airs and during that year participated in a total of 26 contest, traveling approximately 18,000 miles to various sections of the country.

The record of the Royal Airs in National Competition is as follows:

American Legion National Contests

Year of 1958	Placed 25th
" " 1959	" 15th
" " 1960	" 5th
" " 1961	" 2nd

Veterans of Foreign Wars National Contests

Year of 1960	Placed 13th
" " 1961	" 7th

The Royal Airs field 58 performing members, made up of a 33 Horn section, 9 Drum section, Drum Major and 15 girl Color Guard.

The 1962 Goodwill Spectacular Program. *Racine Heritage Museum.*

August 11—Music on the March

> *800 Marching Musicians Vie In Racine, Aug. 11*
> *About 800 marching musicians will be performing Saturday, Aug. 11, at Horlick Field in an extravaganza competition sponsored by the Racine Boy Scout Drum and Bugle Corps. The event, featuring 12 drum corps, will last from 6:15–10:30 p.m. It is one of several activities by the Scout Corps this year in commemoration of the corps' 35th anniversary.*
>
> *1st Time in Racine*
> *Several of the performing units will be coming to Racine for the first time, according to C.F. Martin, chairman of the Racine Scout Corps Executive Committee. These include The Golden Buccaneers of Bridgeport, Conn., St. Joseph's Drum and Bugle Corps, Batavia, New York, and the Marion Cadets, Marion, Ohio. Other junior corps which will be judged in competition will include the Maple City Cadets, La Porte, Ind.; Cedarburg Thunderbolts, Cedarburg Wis.; Madison Scout Corps; St. Mathias Cadets, Milwaukee; and Racine YMCA Kilties. Exhibitions will be performed by the Racine Scout Corps, the Racine Junior Scout Corps, the Kiltie Kadets and the Racine American Legion Boys of '76, the only senior corps performing.*
> —Racine Journal Times, *August 5, 1962*

The first of seventeen Music on the March contests sponsored by the Racine Scouts was a great show. At the time, having one corps from out of the area was rare, and this show had two eastern corps: St. Raphael's Golden Buccaneers of Bridgeport, Connecticut, and St. Joseph's of Batavia, New York. This was remarkable in 1962. Attendance was estimated to be four thousand.

Also of note, the show hosted the second appearance of the contrabass in the Midwest; it had first appeared with St. Raphael's the night before in Lakefront Stadium in Kenosha. The only two junior corps to have contras at that time were St. Raphael's and the Garfield Cadets. There was some discussion before the show whether it was legal. St. Raphael's also had brass-colored bugles, something not used by a top junior corps in the Midwest for some time.

Altogether, the show had twelve drum and bugle corps, four of them finalists. And St. Raphael's was good enough to be a finalist; it was edged out of VFW championship finals in 1962 by only four-tenths of a point by the Racine Scouts.

AUGUST 11, 1962—MUSIC ON THE MARCH

1. 79.8 Madison Scouts V6
2. 78.4 Kilties V11
3. 73.6 St. Joseph's of Batavia
4. 72.7 St. Raphael's Golden Buccaneers
5. 68.8 St. Matthias Cadets
6. 61.6 Mercury Thunderbolts
7. 58.8 Marion Cadets
8. 57.5 Maple City Cadets

Exhibition

Boys of '76 .... A2
Racine Scouts.. V12
Kiltie Kadets
Racine Junior Scouts

The Racine Scouts had worn khaki or olive drab Boy Scout uniforms for thirty-five years since the corps was founded in 1927. The white Aussie hats that members wear in the picture below were worn in 1962 and 1963 as a way to add color and some flash. The corps adopted the famous "Chrome

Racine Scouts, 1962. From the Thirty-fifth Anniversary Contest program. *Courtesy of the Racine Scouts.*

Dome" uniforms in 1964 but continued to wear the Boy Scout uniform (with an overseas cap instead of the Aussie hat) in some parades and competitions and in all color guard and small corps competitions through 1968. At some shows, the members voted on which uniform they would wear, and the Boy Scout uniform often won out.

A St. Raphael's Golden Buccaneer Memory

> *I remember the Racine show very well. The crowd was* great*!!!!!!! The city itself had welcomed us with open arms. Horlick Field was a great experience, being in Racine and competing against a couple of Midwest legends on a field that would become legendary.*
>
> *The contra bass was* very *new in 1962. Garfield and St. Raphael's were the first juniors to have them. The USAF Bolling DC corps got one, and Hawthorne had one by season's end. The brass horns were a result of junk bugles we got from St. Vincent's Cadets* [the leading junior drum and bugle corps of the late '40s to late '50s]. *Our priest, Father DeProfio hired Jim Donnelly, St. Vinnie's brass instructor to teach us.*

St. Raphael's Golden Buccaneers publicity photo, 1962. *Racine Heritage Museum.*

He brought along a ton of Vinnie's charts—"War March," "Jamaica," "Papa Loves Mambo," "Moon Over Miami" and a slug more—and we bought a bunch of St. Vinnie's old brass horns. We added to them over the years, with buys from the Bridgeport Troopers senior corps that went bust in 1963, and new horns from Getzen.
—Cliff Richmond, St. Raphael's Golden Buccaneers, 1962; Buglers Hall of Fame, 2005

From the 1962 Music on the March Program

A Brief History of Participating Corps
St. Raphael's Golden Buccaneers—The "Golden Buccaneers" was formed in 1957, by Rev. Louis A. DeProfio. In 1959 they became members of the Yankee Circuit, and in that year an All-Girl Color Guard was formed. On July 8th, 1959 they made their first appearance as a Marching and Maneuvering Drum & Bugle Corp. In 1960, the Corps entered the Greater New York Circuit. In 1961 they traveled over 10,000 miles and along with the states already mentioned the Corps competed in Pa., Delaware, and Miami, Fla. St. Raphael's "Golden Buccaneers" organized in honor of St. John Bosco, Patron Saint of Youth.
St. Joseph's Drum Corps Assn.—St. Joseph's Drum Corps of Batavia, New York was founded in 1931 by the Rev. T. Bernard Kelly, pastor of St. Joseph's Church in Batavia. The corps is celebrating its 31st anniversary this year. It was strictly a parade corps until 1956. In 1960, the corps took its first shot at the V.F.W. Nationals in Detroit, Michigan, and placed 13th out of 23 junior corps. The corps is the 1961 New York State V.F.W. junior champions.
Maple City Cadets—The Maple City Cadets of La Porte, Indiana, is jointly sponsored by the Hamon Gray Post #83, American Legion and the Hubner-Swanson Post #1130, Veterans of Foreign Wars. Organized 1957, won the Indiana American Legion State Championship 1959–1960 and 1961. Won their first V.F.W. State Championship this past June at Evansville, Indiana. Will be appearing in the V.F.W. National Contest this coming August at Minneapolis, Minn.
Marion Ohio Cadets—The Marion Cadets are the Ohio State V.F.W. and American Legion Champions and will participate at the National V.F.W. contest at Minneapolis in August. We have the honor of having the V.F.W. National Drum Major, Dennis Mertes, playing a bugle in our

corps. He won the National Championship last year and on July 6, 1962 started out the season by winning the Ohio State Championship. Corps consists of sixty-one members at the present time.

MADISON SCOUTS CORPS—Sponsored by the Boy Scouts, parents group and the Associated Optimist Clubs of Madison. Corps is celebrating their 22nd year this year. Wins include National Open Class 1954, Wisconsin State V.F.W. 1957, twice winner of Wisconsin Spectacle of Music, Champions at San Francisco 1956, runner-up National V.F.W. Philadelphia 1954 and in Boston in 1955. Second place at the American Legion convention in Los Angeles in 1956. They have appeared in 5 different countries, 37 states in the U.S.A. and 81 communities in Wisconsin.

RACINE YMCA KILTIES—The Racine "Kilts" clad in resplendent blue of the authentic Scotch Andersen plaid surpass any unit in color on the field of competition. Travels thousands of miles every summer to places such as Miami Beach, Minneapolis, Washington, D.C., St. Louis, Detroit, New York, besides touring the mid-west. They have never failed to field a corps that wasn't a crowd pleaser. The "Kilts" are in their 28th year of organization as an affiliate of the Racine YMCA youth program.

ST. MATTHIAS CADETS—St. Matthias Cadets formed in 1955 as a Girl Scout parade corps from the St. Matthias Parish, advancing to a mixed group and under the sponsorship of the Krejci-Braun-Meier V.F.W. Post #7485 of Milwaukee as well as the St. Matthias Parish. First competition during the 1958 season. 1960 found the corps with their first State Jr. V.F.W. Title, class A champions at the Wisconsin Spectacle of music, second place in one national contest. In 1961 from class B to a class A rating in the Badgerland Association. The only two association corps which were undefeated by the Cadets were the Racine Kilties and the Madison Scouts.

MERCURY THUNDERBOLTS—Organized 1953 with the financial assistance of the Mercury Outboard Motors and the Cedarburg High School Student Council. Champions of the State American Legion Open Junior Contest for 4 years, and first place trophy winners of the Flambeau-Rama for 4 years. Two time winner of third place in the International Lions Parade in Chicago. First place in Horicon Marsh Days Contest, in 1960. This year the corps is sporting new uniforms, corps colors of red, royal blue and tomato red.

September 1—Senior Spectacular

Two American Legion senior championship finalist drum and bugle corps appeared in this nine-corps show. The Spirit of St. Louis, which won this show by almost five points, didn't go to the Las Vegas championship or would likely also have been a finalist. Boys of '76, which finished second in Las Vegas, was judged in exhibition and would have won the show by almost four points.

September 1, 1962—Senior Spectacular
1. 69.850 Spirit of St. Louis
2. 64.950 Hamm's Indians..A3
3. 64.000 Skokie Indians
4. 61.175 Winfield Scott Rebels
5. 61.100 Kewanee Black Nights
6. 60.000 Kenosha Kingsmen

Exhibition
(73.600) Boys of '76 ....A2
(63.875) Kiltie Kadets
(57.475) St. Matthias Cadets

Chapter 5

The Troopers Arrive

1963

1963 Statistics

Shows 3
Drum corps performances 35
States represented 6
VFW champion performances........................ 1
Championship finalist performances 7

The year 1963 marked the beginning of a love affair between the Horlick Athletic Field audience and the Casper, Wyoming Troopers. The Troopers had made a few stops in the Midwest in 1962 as part of its VFW nationals trip to Minneapolis. The Troopers came to Horlick Field on its second tour in 1963. The Horlick Field crowd loved the Troopers from the start, and the Troopers kept coming back. The corps performed in Horlick Field nine times between 1963 and 1970. In one show years later, when the then national champion and hometown Kilties beat the Troopers, the Horlick Field audience booed. Horlick Field was essentially the Troopers' home field for seven years and its two VFW national championships. The corps competed more in Horlick Field than anywhere else during that period, including in its own hometown. One could make the argument that Horlick Field was the home field for the VFW national champion drum and bugle corps in five of the seven years between 1964 and 1970, as the Kilties won three titles and the Troopers won two over that period. The Troopers performed in Horlick Field twice in 1970, the year that it won its second title.

July 3—Goodwill Spectacular

The July 3 show had the top three finalists at the 1963 VFW championships, but that is an empty statement. The VFW show was held in Seattle, and few midwestern or eastern corps went. The Racine Scouts took third at VFW in 1963 but would not have made finals, and perhaps not even the top twenty, if every good corps had gone. On the other hand, the six corps that beat the Racine Scouts in this show would likely have made finals had they gone. If that were so, this would have been a six-finalist show.

Nonetheless, this show had the VFW champion Cavaliers for the second straight year, and it had the Troopers. Few in the audience expected much from the Troopers, which had taken twenty-fifth in 1962 VFW prelims, but the novelty of a drum corps from the West was a draw.

The last paragraph of the article below shows the disdain that the Racine drum corps community had for this corps from the West before it came. But the Troopers immediately won the hearts of the Horlick Field crowd. You didn't have to be well known to be liked by the Horlick Field audience. You just had to be good.

> *Wyoming Drum Corps to Compete in Goodwill Spectacular July 3*
> *A Casper, Wyo. drum and bugle corps uniformed as cavalrymen of the 1860s will be one of seven corps competing at the 1963 Goodwill Spectacular Junior Drum Corps Competition…The Wyoming corps, the Troopers, is one of five competing corps which will march in the July 4 parade. Also competing will be the Cavaliers of Chicago, winner of last year's competition and national junior Veterans of Foreign Wars champions. Other competing corps at the July 3 event will be the Royal Airs of Cicero, Ill., which was second in the American Legion's national competition; the Norwood Park, Ill., Imperials, the Madison Scouts, the Racine Scouts and the Racine Kilties.*
>
> *The Racine Scouts and Kilties, the Madison Scouts, the Cavaliers and the Wyoming Troopers are all scheduled to march in the July 4 parade. The Horlick Field event will also include exhibitions by the Kiltie Kadets, the Racine Junior Boy Scouts, the Elks Youth Band and the "Boys of '76," said Ronald Reichert, chairman of the event.*

3d in Nation

Reichert said the Wyoming Troopers, third in national Legion competition last year, proclaim themselves "champions of the western half of the U.S., having met and defeated all corps from the west coast to the Mississippi (this includes lots of wide open spaces, cactus, jack rabbits and a few drum and bugle corps)."

—Racine Journal Times, *June 28, 1963*

The Troopers in Racine's Fourth of July parade, 1963. *Racine Heritage Museum.*

July 3, 1963—Goodwill Spectacular

1. 80.560 Cavaliers..V1
2. 78.965 Royal Airs
3. 78.225 Kilties
4. 75.520 Troopers..V2
5. 75.400 Madison Scouts
6. 74.360 Norwood Park Imperials
7. 71.010 Racine Scouts..V3

Exhibition

Boys of '76 ....A7
Racine Junior Scouts
Kiltie Kadets

As mentioned in the article above, drum corps that appeared in the July 3 show marched in Racine's Fourth of July parade, which, with all the Racine, Kenosha and Milwaukee-area drum and bugle corps that also marched, made the Racine Fourth of July parade one of the biggest drum and bugle corps parades in the country each year. The corps that won the show got to go first in the parade, which meant that it would get through the three-mile parade before it got really hot and could get out of town early. Corps that appeared late in the sometimes four-hour-long parade didn't get to leave until mid- or even late afternoon.

A Trooper Memory

For 100 kids in the Troopers, Horlick Field was a place we had heard so much about, and were excited to see. To actually go to the hometown of the Kilties was exciting, and to perform at Horlick Field was a dream come true. We felt like we had arrived. The one thing that does stand out is the way the Troopers were treated by members of the Kilties, who by the way we were in awe of. They were very accommodating and respectful. Myself, Fred Sanford and a couple of other Troopers were even invited to a family dinner by one of the Kiltie members. It was surprising that beer was sold at the stadium, I do remember that.

—Pete Emmons, Troopers, 1963; Drum Corps Hall of Fame, 1989

August 11—Music on the March

The second Music on the March had fourteen drum and bugle corps and was the largest show to be held in Horlick Field to date. The Kilties did not go to VFW nationals in 1963 but beat the national champion Cavaliers twice during the year, so it was very good. This show was representative of later Music on the March shows. It had a lot of corps and multiple classes of competition but mostly units competing at a lower level. Of the fourteen units in the show, six were from the Milwaukee area and five from Racine. Only one unit was from out of state: the Maple City Cadets from La Porte, Indiana.

August 11, 1963—Music on the March

Class A

1. 85.60 Kilties
2. 81.75 Madison Scouts
3. 76.45 St. Matthias Cadets
4. 66.85 Starlites
4. 66.85 Maple City Cadets
6. 64.55 Mercury Thunderbolts

Class C

1. 55.90 Kiltie Kadets
2. 54.00 Chordaliers
3. 52.50 Madison Junior Scouts
4. 49.15 St. Matthias Preps
5. 41.50 St. Patrick's Imperials

Exhibition

Boys of '76
Racine Scouts...V3
Racine Junior Scouts

August 31—Spectacular II

The Spectacular II was part of a continuing effort by the Boys of '76 to support the senior activity. It was the fourth year in a row that it sponsored a senior contest. The show had the formula of many of the senior contests that Boys of '76 hosted. Because there weren't that many senior units remaining, the show also had junior classes. Of the five senior corps in the show, two made American Legion finals.

Mercy, which won the junior contest at this show over two other Milwaukee units, was a solid drum corps throughout its history and, over the years, beat several better-known corps. Mercy first appeared in Horlick Field in 1952 and appeared three times overall.

TONIGHT

"BOYS of '76"

Racine American Legion Drum Corps

PRESENTS

1963 Spectacular II

Senior and Junior

DRUM AND BUGLE CORPS

COMPETITION

7 P.M.

Horlick Athletic Field

SEE THESE DRUM CORPS IN COMPETITION

CLASS A	*CLASS B*	*CLASS B*
Spirit of St. Louis	Starlights—Milwaukee	Racine Kiltie Kadets
The Kenosha Kingsmen	Mercy High—Milwaukee	Racine Jr. Scout Corps
The Skokie Indians	Militaires—Milwaukee	
Hamm's Indians—Minneapolis		

EXHIBITIONS BY

Racine Kiltie Drum & Bugle Corps

Boys of '76 Drum & Bugle Corps

HELP SEND THE "BOYS OF '76" TO THE NATIONAL CONVENTION

Admission: Adults—$1.50

Children—(under 15 years)—75c

(under 8 years)—Free

August 31, 1963—Spectacular II

Class A

1. 79.9 Spirit of St. Louis..A8
2. 78.0 Skokie Indians
3. 75.8 Hamm's Indians
4. 73.2 Kenosha Kingsmen

Class B

1. 78.8 Mercy High School All-girl
2. 73.4 Starlites
3. 59.0 Militaires

Class C

1. 69.3 Kiltie Kadets
2. 69.0 Racine Junior Scouts

Exhibition

Boys of '76 ....A7
Kilties

Chapter 6

The Second-Best Show Ever Held in Horlick Athletic Field

1964

1964 Statistics

Shows	3
Drum corps performances	33
States represented	6
VFW champion performances	3
Championship finalist performances	10

In the winter and spring of 1963–64, Racine rebuilt Horlick Athletic Field, replacing the thirty-nine-year-old baseball field layout with a more modern, but compact, football field and grandstands and a separate baseball field. This change is what truly made Horlick Field a special place for drum and bugle corps and audiences. Before, the football field had stretched across the outfield and part of the infield of the baseball field, and fans sat on low bleachers in the outfield or far away in the diagonally facing covered bleachers.

The new grandstands were only a few feet from the field, with barely enough room for the tabulation table, and five feet up. Performers and audience could make eye contact and direct, personal connections not allowed in stadiums with tracks. The audience was so close that it could, and often did, talk to performers on the field. Performers could see the excitement in the eyes of the people in the crowd, and the thrill it generated in performers led to powerful, emotional performances that many still recall today as their best moment in drum corps.

Another aspect of the compact arrangement of Horlick Field's football field helped to make it unique. The grandstands went from end zone to end zone and left only a few yards between the grandstands and the concession stand. This area was always congested with people in line for food, standing by the field's boundary fence and watching the corps on the field or moving between the bleachers and the concession stand; and with the next corps lined up, waiting to enter the field. Drum Corps Hall of Fame member Ken Norman called it the Reception Line.

Corps members who stood waiting to go on or were moving onto the field rubbed elbows and bodies with the audience and sometimes had liquids or food spilled on them. The crowd got to see each corps up close, as individual young people, energized to go on. Former corps members, many with beers, watched closely, looking into the faces and talking to the members as they stood waiting or as they marched onto the field. Fans could see, face to face, that some corps were hyped to the point of hyperventilating and that others were calm and relaxed, so the fans knew in advance which corps were going to try to light them up. It added to the personal connection of the audience and corps members and the anticipation and appreciation of great performances.

The redesign also had the people in the concert-side bleachers face the foundries across the street.

July 3—East-West Spectacular

10 Corps Compete July 3 for $5,000 in Prizes
Ten drum and bugle corps from the northern United States and Ontario, Canada, will compete in the annual Junior Drum and Bugle Corps competition July 3 at Horlick Athletic Field, as a prelude to the Racine July 4 Goodwill parade. More than $5,000 in prizes will be awarded in the competition which Ollie Johnson, general chairman of the event, called "the biggest one ever attempted that I know of in the state of Wisconsin."

$1,200 First Prize
Corps from Chicago, Madison, Toronto, Boston, Racine and Casper, Wyo., will compete for the first prize of $1,200, and ten other prizes. Mayor William H. Beyer has announced that the drum corps competition will include a formal dedication of the remodeled Horlick Field.

The ten competing corps are: The Cavaliers, Chicago, Ill., a 16-year-old 80-member corps which is the current national drum and bugle corps champion, and the only Midwest junior corps to win a major national title, which it has done five times. The Toronto Optimists Drum Corps, Canadian junior champions since 1958. The Troopers from Casper, Wyo., currently holds second place in the Veterans of Foreign Wars national competition and their color guard is current national champion. The corps wears the uniform of the cavalry of the 1860s. The Crusaders from Boston, Mass. This corps won the New England States championship and the Northeastern States championship in 1957 and 1958. They won the Eastern Massachusetts championship in those same years, and again in 1963, and placed fifth in the first annual World Open competition last year.

Norwood Park, Ill., Imperials have won six state titles since 1954 and ranked in the top ten of every national championship they have attended. The corps includes a 16-girl color guard. Racine Kilties were 1963 Wisconsin State American Legion Junior Open champions and were named Wisconsin's top drum corps last year. Spartans, from Morton Grove, Ill., a new 72-member corps will compete in Racine for the first time as a unit. Chicago's Royal Airs are consistent winners in the Chicago area and have played in Racine competitions previously. The Racine Explorer Scout Corps, organized in 1927, is known as scouting's oldest musical unit. It has won five national championships and has performed at the 1933 World's Fair and the 1937 National Scout Jamboree in Washington, D.C. More than 5,000 Racine boys have been members of the corps in its 37-year history…The Madison Explorer Scouts were organized in 1938 and have traveled to five foreign countries and 42 states. The corps played at the 1947 Boy Scout World Jamboree in Molsson, France, and is consistently among the top 10 corps in national competition.

—Racine Journal Times, *June 25, 1964*

The 1964 East-West Spectacular was perhaps the biggest show the Midwest had ever seen outside of nationals competitions and was the third-best drum corps show of the entire year after VFW Nationals and the World Open: it had the corps that finished first, second, third, fourth, eleventh and thirteenth at VFW nationals and the Canadian champion. In comparison, CYO Nationals that year had the corps that finished fourth, fifth, ninth and twelfth and no Canadian corps. The Dream had only the corps that finished fifth, seventh, eighth and twelfth. The *Racine Journal Times* reported that 7,200 people attended the show.

MAKE YOUR "FOURTH" WEEK END IN RACINE COMPLETE

START JULY 3rd AND THRILL AT THE

RACINE 'BOYS OF '76'

EAST-WEST

SPECTACULAR!

TEN INTERNATIONALLY KNOWN DRUM and BUGLE CORPS

COMPETING FOR TOP HONORS

7:00 p.m. at the New Horlick Athletic Field

BIGGEST EVENT OF ITS KIND in the HISTORY OF RACINE'S 'BOYS OF '76'!

Selected champions from U.S. and Canada will compete against Racine's Kilties and Explorer's Drum and Bugle Corps.

JUDGED BY PROFESSIONALS FROM ALL OVER THE NATION

100 MINUTES FROM THE NATION'S BEST!

A 10 Minute Performance Each From:

- Cavaliers, Park Ridge, Ill.
- Madison Scouts, Madison, Wis.
- Spartans, Morton Grove, Ill.
- Boston Crusaders, Boston, Mass.
- Toronto Optimists, Toronto, Ontario
- Golden Troopers, Casper, Wyo.
- Imperials, Norwood Park, Ill.
- Royal-Airs, Chicago, Ill.
- KILTIES, Racine, Wis.
- EXPLORERS, Racine, Wis.

ADMISSION

Reserved Seats $2.50

General Admission $1.50

Children $1.00

MORE THAN $5,000.00 in Prize Money

TOP PRIZE, $1,200

Purchase your advance tickets today!
Write for, or call on:

DRAEGER STEREO & CAMERA CENTER
1919 Taylor Ave.

RONSHOLT'S 5c to $1.00 STORE
1502 Washington Ave.

WIEGAND BROS. JEWELRY & MUSIC STORE
420 Main St.

BEZUCHA JEWELERS
1671 Douglas Ave.

JOHNSON'S MUSIC, INC.
1409 Washington Ave.

TURNSTYLE FAMILY CENTER
4901 Washington Ave.

OR

Write to P.O. Box 76, Racine, Wis.

SPECIAL!

MAYOR WILLIAM H. BEYER

has announced that the official dedication of the NEW Horlick Field will take place at this event—prompty at 7 p.m.

Racine Scouts performing its version of the flag raising on Iwo Jima in the new "Chrome Dome" uniforms, 1964. *Courtesy of Ron Da Silva.*

This was a must-see show for many reasons. It had the top eastern corps, the top western corps, the top Canadian corps and the top three corps from the Midwest. It was also the first appearance in Racine of the new Racine Scout uniform, which had been developed in complete secrecy; the members had been ordered to not describe it to anyone. The Racine Scouts had worn olive drab Boy Scout uniforms for thirty-seven years since it had been formed. The word was that the new uniform was something completely different. It was supposed to have been delivered before the beginning of the season but was delayed. It was first worn at the Cedarburg Music Festival in late June. The suspense of what the new uniform was like was almost as big a draw as the competing drum corps to the Horlick Field Audience, and it added to the excitement leading up to the July 3, 1964 show. The first appearance of the uniform in Racine was a special moment for the corps and the audience, a sizable portion of which had worn the olive drab. The new, shiny chrome helmets lit up the night and the audience.

In a very competitive year for drum corps, the Racine Scouts tied the PAL Cadets of Bridgeport, Connecticut, for thirteenth place at the 1964 VFW prelims. However, a tabulation error was later found in Garfield Cadets's score sheet that would have dropped Garfield several places and put the Racine Scouts and PAL into finals tied for twelfth place. Personal accounts claim as fact that Garfield knew of the error but did not tell anyone until after finals, ensuring its performance in finals and keeping the Scouts and PAL from finals appearances that they had earned. If Garfield had reported the error, this would have been another seven-finalist show.

July 3, 1964—East-West Spectacular

1. 77.40 Boston Crusaders V4
2. 75.50 Royal Airs... V2
3. 73.90 Cavaliers.. V3
4. 72.40 Kilties V1
5. 66.30 Norwood Park Imperials
6. 66.20 Racine Scouts
7. 64.80 Troopers... V11
8. 62.50 Morton Grove Spartans
9. 61.75 Toronto Optimists
10. 58.35 Madison Scouts

Exhibition

Boys of '76 .... A3

In the *Drum Corps World* article that follows, Boston Crusaders' 1964 corps manager, Joseph Dowling, writes of the "long and arduous trip" to Racine. It highlights how rare a tour was for a drum and bugle corps at the time and how difficult it seemed for the corps and performers:

> *Crusaders win Big One*
> *Appearing in the "East-West Spectacular" held in Racine, Wisconsin the evening of July 3, 1964, the Boston Crusaders drum & bugle corps toppled the drum corps giants of the Midwest and Canada in decisive fashion after a long and arduous trip from Boston. In the Top Junior contest of the Midwest this season the Crusaders defeated the current Jr. V.F.W. National Champions the Chicago Cavaliers and at the same time sent down to defeat the Canadian Jr. Champions the Toronto Optimists. The Crusaders placed first with a point score of 77.4 and second was the Royal Airs of Chicago with a score of 75.5, third was the Chicago Cavaliers with a point score of 73.35 and way down in 9th position were the Toronto Optimists with a score of 61.75. In so doing the boys from the New Boston Took home with them the $1,200 first place prize money.*

In capturing the East-West Spectacular, the Boston Crusaders have now defeated all of the current Jr. Champions in the United States and Canada during the 1964 Season.

In the Racine Contest, the Crusaders put on one of the most exciting and explosive performances in their long and colorful career and amazed all of the Wisconsin fans with their excellent program. A standing ovation was accorded the Crusaders as they appeared in the Grand Finale for the presentation of prizes. A fine example of the sportsmanship prevalent in Drum corps was manifested by the other competing corps when they serenaded the Crusaders after the prizes were announced. After the contest literally hundreds of members of the other corps went out of their way to express their congratulations to the members of the Crusaders.
Joseph F. Dowling, Mgr., Boston Crusaders Drum & Bugle Corps
—Drum Corps World, *December 1964*

Mr. Dowling entered the Massachusetts Drum Corps and Music Educators Hall of Fame in 1995.

A Boston Crusader Memory

The Midwest trip was a huge undertaking for the Crusaders. Out of state trips were rare and local circuit contests were the norm. Thus, the combination of a fast start and the timing of the trip gave the Crusaders a once in a lifetime opportunity to establish themselves as a National Champion contender with this scheduled trip into the heart of Midwest drum corps.

The 1964 Crusaders had clearly identified themselves as the top eastern corps as the date for the Midwest invasion approached. However, the consensus was that the chances of actually winning out there seemed remote and the goal seemed to center on performing well and continuing to improve. In fact historically in previous years Eastern powerhouses such as SAC and Garfield had made similar trips and returned empty handed.

The undefeated Cavaliers were on the field when the Crusaders arrived at the field. When the Cavies began their exit to the strains of "Over the Rainbow," the Boston Crusaders realized this was the big time and the opportunity was close at hand. The Crusaders performed their fast-paced (140 cadence), GE-packed routine dramatically different from the execution-focused competition of the Midwest powers of the time. The

Boston Crusaders, 1964 Goodwill Spectacular Program. *Racine Heritage Museum.*

response from the Racine crowd was incredible and the Crusaders were the subject of a sustained standing ovation as the corps performed their exit from the field. The up close stands and the packed in crowd contributed to the reaction to our show that night.

When the Kilties were announced fourth, an audible gasp rose from the crowd. The Crusaders were still in it! Next score announced in third were the undefeated National Champion Cavaliers and the gasp from the crowd was even louder. Next to us on the field a member of the Royal Airs yelled over for a reaction towards the win over the Cavies. The Crusaders never moved and a moment later it was the Royal Airs who were announced in second. The crowd went berserk as the Crusaders remained at parade rest not a member moving an inch. The Crusader score was announced and it turned out to be a comfortable two point win. The crowd, perhaps realizing the historical result remained buzzing for minutes after the scores.

It was later learned that arch rival St. Kevin's had gathered at their corps hall awaiting a call with the scores on what was sure to be a Crusader crushing defeat. When the call finally came in from Racine and the scores read the hall emptied in stunned silence. Days later Drum Corps News *headlined with "Crusaders top Cavs, Royal Airs in Midwest Invasion."*

The Crusaders, still high from the night before, proudly marched in the Racine Fourth of July parade, receiving an unbelievable response along the route of the parade. Everywhere we went while in Racine we were greeted by friendly knowledgeable drum corps fans. Returning to Boston, the Crusaders were treated as conquering heroes by fans everywhere.

Forty eight years later it remains the single greatest win in the long history of the Boston Crusaders. When the old grey alumni get together this show is always brought up. I'm sure in 2014 the current Boston Crusaders will do something to recognize that event on the 50th anniversary.

—John Sullivan, Boston Crusaders, 1964; Massachusetts Drum Corps and Music Educators Hall of Fame, 2000

A Toronto Optimists Memory

This was our first trip to Racine. The stadium was perfect for a drum corps show and the evening crowd was very free with their applause during our performance. I'll always remember the crowd applause. I think we finished ninth or tenth which was disappointing and, since we weren't allowed to "boo" the result, it was nice that the crowd generously "booed" the result loudly for us.

—Vern Johansson, Toronto Optimists, 1964

Toronto Optimists, 1964 Goodwill Spectacular Program. *Racine Heritage Museum.*

This account is evidence of what others have noted: the Horlick Field audience made its feelings known. While the audience was free with raucous standing ovations, it enjoyed booing, too.

The 1964 East-West Spectacular put Horlick Field on the map. It was reported in almost every drum and bugle corps periodical, and the Boston Crusaders carried the word personally to the East. Afterward, Horlick Field was known throughout the activity for its great audience, tough competition, big prize money and wonderful environment.

July 28—Roland Olson Memorial Concert

The drum and bugle corps activity, by its nature, puts many men, women and children on the road each summer. Since the activity began, men and women have judged contests until late at night and then have gotten into their cars to drive home, sometimes for hours along dark, narrow roads.

Roland Olson was a well-known and highly respected music teacher in Racine who was deeply involved in drum corps and other forms of music in Racine. Late at night on his way home after judging a drum and bugle corps contest in 1963, he died in an automobile accident. This show was held to honor his memory and as a benefit for his family. The Racine Scouts, Racine Junior Scouts, Kilties, Kiltie Kadets, Boys of '76 and Elks Youth Band performed along with two choruses, two high school bands and the Johnson's Wax Band. It was interrupted but not stopped by rain.

> *Storm Halts Memorial Concert*
> *The haunting refrain, "When you walk through a storm, keep your chin up high..." floated across Horlick Field Tuesday night as lightning crackled and rain began to fall on 2,000 spectators...The audience shrunk rapidly as the rainstorms grew worse...However, an unexpected climax to the program was provided by the YMCA Kilties who insisted on paying tribute to Olson despite the nearly empty stadium and a steady drizzle. The 70-member drum corps donned raincoats, marched onto the field and boomed out with rollicking Scottish tunes in the rain.*
> —Racine Journal Times, *July 29, 1964*

July 28, 1964—Roland Olson Memorial Concert
All Exhibition

Kilties V1
Racine Scouts
Boys of '76 .... A3
Kiltie Kadets
Racine Junior Scouts

August 8—Music on the March

> *Scout Corps to Stage Field Show Aug. 8*
> *A Japanese-American drum and bugle corps from Chicago will be among 18 corps performing at Horlick Field on Saturday, Aug. 8, in a "Music on the March" competition presented by the Racine Scout Parents Club.*
> *The Japanese-American corps, called the Nisei Ambassadors, is comprised mainly of children whose fathers served in the famed 442d Combat Team of the American Army…* [which] *served with distinction in Europe during World War II and became the most decorated outfit in the American Army during the war. The Nisei drum corps includes a 20-girl color guard among its 63 members. It will be the corps' first appearance in Racine.*
> *The show will begin at 6 p.m. on Aug. 8 with exhibitions by six corps—the Boys of '76, Elks Youth Band, Junior Boy Scout Drum and Bugle Corps, Racine Explorer Scouts, Rookie Scout Corps and the Ambassa-Dears, an all-girl corps. At 6:30 p.m. the competition will get underway with five corps performing in Class "C"—the Nisei Ambassadors of Chicago, Boy Scouts of Madison, St. Matthias Preps of Milwaukee, Kiltie Kadets of Racine and St. Patrick's Imperials of Milwaukee.*
> *This will be followed by Class "A" competition with the Vanguards of Skokie, Ill., the Brigade of Highland Park, Ill., the Cadets of Cedar Rapids, Iowa, the Explorer Scouts of Madison, St. Mathias Cadets of Milwaukee, Mercury Thunderbolts of Cedarburg, Wis., and YMCA Kilties of Racine.*
> —Racine Journal Times, *July 29, 1964*

For the second year in a row, Music on the March set a record for most drum and bugle corps in a show in Horlick Field. But it was a pedestrian show, with only two finalists appearing: the national champion Kilties and the Boys of '76, which took third at American Legion. Of the seventeen drum corps in the show, only four were from out of state. All seven Racine drum corps and the Elks Youth Band appeared in the show. At this time, the Racine Scouts had three competing units, one each in A, B and C class.

Custer's Brigade was a mid-level Chicago-area drum corps that wore Trooper-like uniforms and folded at the end of the year. The Cedar Rapids Cadets, formed in 1928, competed against the Racine Scouts at the Chicagoland Music Festivals in the early 1930s and was one of the first drum corps to adopt the valved bugle. The *Racine Journal Times* reported that three thousand people were in the audience.

August 8, 1964—Music on the March*

Class A

1. Kilties V1
2. Skokie Vanguard
3. St. Matthias Cadets

Madison Scouts
Custer's Brigade
Cedar Rapids Cadets
Mercury Thunderbolts

Class C

Nisei Ambassadors
Madison Junior Scouts
St. Matthias Preps
Kiltie Kadets
St. Patrick's Imperials

Exhibition

Boys of '76 .... A3
Racine Scouts
Racine Junior Scouts
Racine Rookie Scouts
AmbassaDears

*Places after the top three and all scores are unknown.

Chapter 7

The Most Corps Performances in One Year

1965

1965 Statistics

Number of shows..4
Drum corps performances............................47
States represented..9
Championship finalist performances.............5

If you liked to see a lot of drum and bugle corps, Horlick Athletic Field in 1965 was the place for you. Horlick Field hosted four drum corps shows and forty-seven drum and bugle corps performances. The Racine Scouts' Music on the March alone had twenty-five corps; it started in the morning with a Class C competition and had a parade in the afternoon and a Class A competition at night.

Boys of '76 was doing its best to promote the dying Midwest senior activity. It sponsored two senior competitions in 1965 for a total of six senior contests between 1960 and 1965. Maumee Demons, Kenosha Kingsmen, Boys of '76 and Men of Brass appeared in both shows in 1965.

June 7—Drum Corps Day

The year 1965 was the only one in which Racine's unique Drum Corps Day exhibition was held in Horlick Field. In other years, it was held in

Pershing Park on the lakefront. Drum Corps Day was held each year to celebrate Racine's drum and bugle corps heritage and its many drum corps. The Racine drum corps and Elks Youth Band all performed at the free exhibition show. In some years, corps from Kenosha and the Milwaukee area also performed.

June 7, 1965—Drum Corps Day
Exhibition
Racine Junior Scouts
Kiltie Kadets
AmbassaDears
Racine Scouts
Kilties V3
Kenosha Kingsmen

> *5,000 watch drum corps—Color guard units from five Racine drum and bugle corps and the Elks Youth Band massed on Horlick Field Thursday night prior to performing before an estimated 5,000 spectators. The exhibition was part of Racine's second annual Drum Corps Day celebration…A surprise visitor was Tony Schlecta, permanent chairman of the national VFW drum corps competition which will be held at Chicago Aug. 18 this year. "I'm greatly impressed by the number of fine drum corps in a city the size of Racine," Schlecta commented.*
> *—caption from the* Racine Journal Times, *June 19, 1965*

July 4—Goodwill Spectacular

The July 4 show had five senior and two junior corps competing. Both junior corps made VFW finals that year, but none of the five seniors in the show did. Maumee Demons, making its first appearance in Horlick Field, won its first of three straight Horlick Field contests.

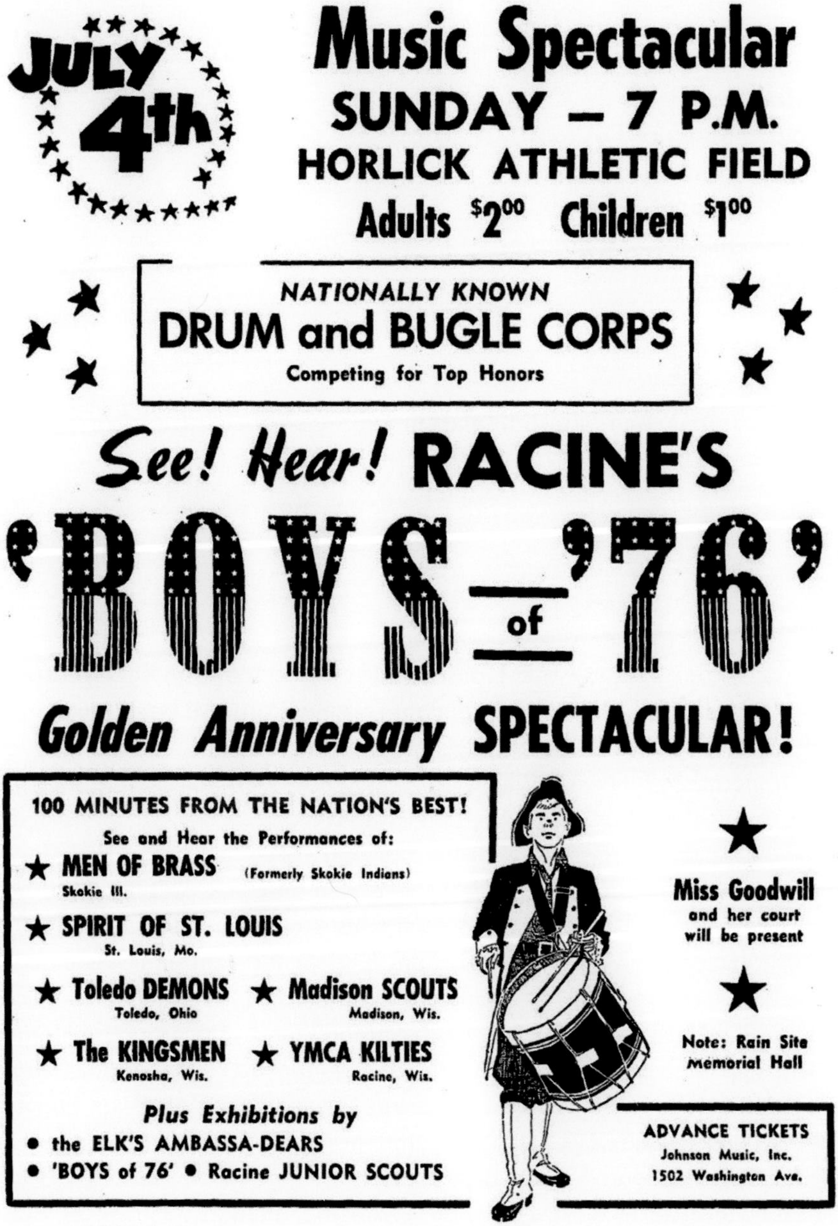
JULY 4th
Music Spectacular
SUNDAY – 7 P.M.
HORLICK ATHLETIC FIELD
Adults $2.00 Children $1.00
NATIONALLY KNOWN
DRUM and BUGLE CORPS
Competing for Top Honors
See! Hear! RACINE'S
'BOYS of '76'
Golden Anniversary SPECTACULAR!
100 MINUTES FROM THE NATION'S BEST!
See and Hear the Performances of:
★ MEN OF BRASS (Formerly Skokie Indians)
Skokie Ill.
★ SPIRIT OF ST. LOUIS
St. Louis, Mo.
★ Toledo DEMONS
Toledo, Ohio
★ Madison SCOUTS
Madison, Wis.
★ The KINGSMEN
Kenosha, Wis.
★ YMCA KILTIES
Racine, Wis.
Plus Exhibitions by
• the ELK'S AMBASSA-DEARS
• 'BOYS of 76' • Racine JUNIOR SCOUTS
Miss Goodwill
and her court
will be present
Note: Rain Site
Memorial Hall
ADVANCE TICKETS
Johnson Music, Inc.
1502 Washington Ave.

July 4, 1965—Goodwill Spectacular

Junior

1. 86.483 Kilties V3
2. 82.550 Madison Scouts V14*

Senior

1. 75.600 Maumee Demons
2. 74.800 Kenosha Kingsmen
3. 72.133 Men of Brass senior
4. 70.933 Spirit of St. Louis

Exhibition

Boys of '76
Racine Junior Scouts
AmbassaDears

*VFW national championship finals in 1965 had fifteen drum corps, three more than usual.

August 14—Music on the March

This was the largest show that Horlick Field ever hosted, with fifteen corps in Class C and ten in Class A. It had ten out-of-state drum and bugle corps from eight different states. But only one was a championship finalist: Norwood Park Imperials, which won this show by six points, took tenth at VFW.

Music on the March by now had established a personality. While the Goodwill Spectacular usually hosted the best corps, Music on the March hosted a lot of drum corps from a lot of different places. This show had fifteen corps from Wisconsin; two each from Iowa, Michigan and Illinois; and one each from Minnesota, Missouri, Kansas and Louisiana. The *Racine Journal Times* reported the attendance as six thousand.

The 1965 Music on the March was Norwood's ninth appearance in Horlick Field (it appeared thirteen times in total) and was the first of two straight Music on the March victories. Norwood was at the Twenty-fifth Anniversary Show in 1952 and last appeared as the Skokie Imperials in 1976.

The Racine Scouts Junior corps was a big, talented unit that competed at Class B level and won several contests in 1965, including some over Class A corps. In an annual senior versus junior corps full dress competition judged by instructors in early August, the junior corps was said to have beaten the senior corps. The senior corps then moved about ten of the

The Racine Junior Scouts in a Racine parade, 1965. *Photo by Bud House, courtesy of Sandy House.*

St. Paul Scouts publicity photo, 1965. *From the collection of* Drum Corps World.

best junior corps' horns and drums to the senior corps for the remainder of the season.

The Stardusters had a Racine connection. The corps was founded in 1961 by Charles Dadian, former business manager for the Boys of '76, when his job moved him to New Orleans. The Stardusters, based 1,100 miles away, appeared in Horlick Field four times between 1965 and 1971.

St. Paul Scouts was an excellent unit that performed mostly in Minnesota, Wisconsin and the Upper Peninsula. It was always big and entertaining. SPS, as many in the local area referred to the corps, was based almost four hundred miles away but performed in Horlick Field six times between 1965 and 1972.

The AmbassaDears was formed in 1964 and first performed field shows in 1965. The corps performed several times each year in Horlick Field. Its most competitive years were 1970 and 1971, when it placed third and fifth in Class A/All-Girl competition at the U.S. Open. In retrospect, the AmbassaDears may have been the luckiest drum corps members in Racine. They were at almost every big show in Horlick Field history, where they put on an early exhibition and then went into the stands and watched all the great corps. Members of the Kilties and Racine Scouts, who either competed or performed exhibitions after the others had performed, didn't see nearly as many of the great corps as did the AmbassaDears.

August 14, 1965—Music on the March

Class C

1. 74.15 Kenosha Shoreliners
2. 73.90 St. Patrick's Imperials
3. 69.30 Mercury Thunderbolts

Kenosha Queensmen*
Chevaliers of Waterloo
Kiltie Kadets
Cedar Rapids Grenadiers
Oshkosh Warriors
Guardsmen
AmbassaDears
Belles of St. Mary's
Gladiators
Chordaliers
St. Matthias Preps
St. Gregory's Crusaders
*Remaining scores and places are unknown.

Class A
1. 83.80 Norwood Park Imperials................................V10
2. 78.00 St. Paul Scouts
3. 75.95 American Woodman Cadets
4. 73.25 Ishpeming Blue Notes
5. 72.90 Sky Ryders
6. 70.95 Northernaires
7. 68.50 St. Matthias Cadets
8. 67.00 Stardusters

Exhibition
Racine Scouts
Racine Junior Scouts

A Norwood Park Imperial Memory

The Norwood Park Imperials marched in Horlick Field for many years. The stadium was old and the crowd was really close *to the field, the performance became very* personal*! for everyone. The crowd was a real drum corps crowd. The contests were always well attended and were usually very competitive shows due to the choice of corps asked to attend.*

I remember that you could buy beer at the field. That made it a great place for the older corps members. After all, the age was only 18 then! Also, the audience seemed to be "happier" there. At least until the contest results were announced!

—David Borck, Norwood Park Imperials, 1965

SEPTEMBER 5—MIDWEST SENIOR CHAMPIONSHIPS

Seven senior corps from six states appeared in this show, five of them for the second time in Horlick Field in 1965. Only Hamm's Indians, which took fourth in this show, was a national contest finalist: it placed fourth at American Legion nationals in 1965.

It is likely that a few of Racine's six junior corps performed exhibitions at this show, but no record of an exhibition unit was found.

MIDWEST SENIOR
ASSOCIATION

HORLICK FIELD
Racine
SUNDAY, SEPT. 5
8:00 P.M.

DRUM & BUGLE PAGEANTRY
of
SENIORS on the SPOT

FIRST ALL-MIDWEST SENIOR CHAMPIONSHIP COMPETITION

★ **BOYS OF '76**

38 times state champion, celebrating their golden anniversary in 1965. One of the nation's first senior corps.

★ **KINGSMEN**

1965 Wisconsin Legion and V.F.W. champs, known as one of the midwest's sharpest marching and maneuvering corps.

★ **MEN OF BRASS**

Based at McHenry, Ill., the Men of Brass march their precision drill to a Dixieland beat. "St. James Infirmary" is one of their best.

★ **SPIRIT OF ST. LOUIS**

The songs of the old Mississippi River steamboats, kept alive by the Negro's innate love of jazz music. A favorite of Racine crowds.

★ **MAUMEE DEMONS**

Ohio state champions and one of the Midwest's winningest senior corps in 1965. They march to the hit music of Broadway.

★ **HAMM'S INDIANS**

From the Land of Sky Blue Waters comes the only drum corps ever to lead a Rose Bowl parade. Authentic Indian costumes add color to their show.

★ **GOVENAIRES**

1965 Legion State Champions from St. Peter, Minn. Always a crowd-pleaser.

★ **VANGUARD**

From St. Clair Shores, just outside Detroit, comes Michigan's contender for the Midwest senior crown.

ADULTS $1.50 **UNDER 14, $1.00**

September 5, 1965—Midwest Senior Championships

1. 61.22 Maumee Demons
2. 59.40 Kenosha Kingsmen
3. 57.28 Boys of '76
4. 54.35 Hamm's Indians..A4
5. 47.07 Men of Brass senior
6. 43.65 Spirit of St. Louis
7. 35.03 St. Clair Shores Vanguard

Exhibition

Unknown

Chapter 8

The Fight for Finals

1966

1966 Statistics

Number of shows..2
Drum corps performances..........................28
States represented 8
Championship finalist performances 7

In 1966, Horlick Field was the battleground for four very good drum and bugle corps that were fighting to establish dominance and ensure a spot in the VFW national finals contest: Kilties, Norwood Park Imperials, Madison Scouts and Racine Scouts. The four corps traded victories all season. At any of the shows in which the corps competed, any of them could have come out on top. Based on the nationwide strength of drum and bugle corps competition in the summer of 1966, the corps that finished the lowest, and perhaps the two lowest, of the four at VFW prelims was likely to miss finals. In this competitive environment, the shows were stellar.

The highest-placing corps that appeared in Horlick Field in 1966 was the Kilties, which finished eighth at VFW Nationals. The Kilties, Racine Scouts, Madison Scouts, Racine Junior Scouts, Kenosha Queensmen, Kiltie Kadets and AmbassaDears appeared in both shows.

July 3—Goodwill Spectacular

The 1966 Goodwill Spectacular continued to support the senior activity by hosting the eighth senior competition in Horlick Field in seven years. Of the four junior units competing in this show, the three eventual VFW championship finalist units each thought they should win this show and put on a performance to make it so. The finishing order was the Kilties, Madison Scouts and Racine Scouts—the same order that they would place at VFW nationals the following month.

With this year's win in the senior class, the Maumee Demons had now won three straight senior contests in Horlick Field. It was to be the last senior contest held in Horlick Field for nine years. In a few short years, the senior activity had all but disappeared in the Midwest.

July 3, 1966—Goodwill Spectacular

Junior

1. 71.716 Kilties V8
2. 70.716 Madison Scouts V10
3. 70.588 Racine Scouts V13*
4. 55.266 St. Matthias Cadets

Senior

1. 66.85 Maumee Demons
2. 49.83 Kenosha Kingsmen
3. 44.86 Spirit of St. Louis

Exhibition

Boys of '76
Racine Junior Scouts
AmbassaDears
Kiltie Kadets
Kenosha Queensmen

*Because of a controversy regarding one drum corps' penalty in prelims, VFW nationals had thirteen finalists in 1966.

JULY 4th
Music Spectacular
SUNDAY – 7:30 P.M.
HORLICK ATHLETIC FIELD
Adults $2.00 Children $1.00
NATIONALLY KNOWN
DRUM and BUGLE CORPS
Competing for Top Honors
See! Hear!
150 Minutes from THE NATION'S BEST !
The Performance of:
★ St. Mathias Cadets
Milwaukee
★ Spirit of St. Louis
St. Louis, Mo.
★ Toledo Demons
Toledo, Ohio
★ Madison Scouts
Madison
★ The Kingsmen
Kenosha
★ YMCA Kilties
Racine
★ Explorer Scouts
Racine
Miss Goodwill and her court will be present
Note: Rain Site Memorial Hall
Plus Exhibitions by
★ Kenosha Queensmen
★ Boys of '76
★ Racine Kiltie Kadets
★ The Elks
★ Racine Scout Corps
Advance Tickets Available at Johnson Music, Inc. – 1502 Wash. Ave.

AUGUST 13—MUSIC ON THE MARCH

The 1966 Music on the March had sixteen corps in two classes. It was the second show of the year in Horlick Field that had three VFW finalists that were closely competitive all year and competing for the last few spots in VFW finals, now just two weeks away. They all had statements to make. Norwood Park won this show by 1.9 points over the Kilties and 2.7 points over the Madison Scouts but lost to both corps two weeks later at VFW nationals. The Racine Scouts, another corps in the same competitive group, was in judged exhibition.

The show was also one of the several shows during the summer of 1966 in which all three Scout corps appeared: the Racine, Madison and St. Paul Scouts. All were big, entertaining corps, and any of them could have come out on top at any show during the summer. Along with the Kilties, the four all-boy corps traded victories all summer as they dominated Wisconsin competition.

In all, sixteen corps from eight states and Canada were in the show, and four of them were finalists. The show had one corps each from Canada, Ohio, Illinois and Minnesota and two from Iowa. It had eight all-boy corps and three all-girl corps.

Madison Scouts, 1966. Madison Scouts wore this dark green cadet uniform between 1962 and 1966. *Courtesy of Ron Da Silva.*

August 13, 1966—Music on the March

Class A

1. 76.4 Norwood Park Imperials V12
2. 74.5 Kilties V8
3. 73.7 Madison Scouts V10
4. 67.9 St. Paul Scouts
5. 61.0 Sarnia Sertomanaires
6. 52.8 Kenosha Queensmen
7. 51.6 Sandusky Eaglettes
8. 51.2 Cedar Rapids Grenadiers

Class C

1. 68.7 Fort Dodge Lancers
2. 60.2 St. Gregory's Crusaders
3. 59.9 Belles of St. Mary's
4. 58.5 Kiltie Kadets
5. 47.6 Madison Junior Scouts
6. 43.0 AmbassaDears

Exhibition

Racine Scouts V13*

Racine Junior Scouts

*VFW nationals had thirteen finalists in 1966.

Chapter 9

The Big Upset

1967

1967 Statistics

Number of shows..2
Drum corps performances............................25
States represented 7
Championship finalist performances 9

Both shows in 1967 were upsets. The first was one of the biggest upsets ever. People still talk—and sometimes argue—about it.

July 3—Goodwill Spectacular

The 1967 Goodwill Spectacular was, without question, a big upset; it remains today a topic of conversation. It was one of the toughest shows in Horlick Field history. It had six VFW finalists, including five of the top six corps: the Royal Airs, Des Plaines Vanguard, Casper Troopers, Racine Kilties and Racine Scouts.

From 1927 when it was formed, the Racine Scouts had been one of the best drum and bugle corps in the country, going undefeated for years in the 1930s, playing on television and radio and traveling nationwide. It remained strongly competitive through the 1950s but, by the 1960s, was a milestone for making finals. Corps that beat the Racine Scouts made finals (between

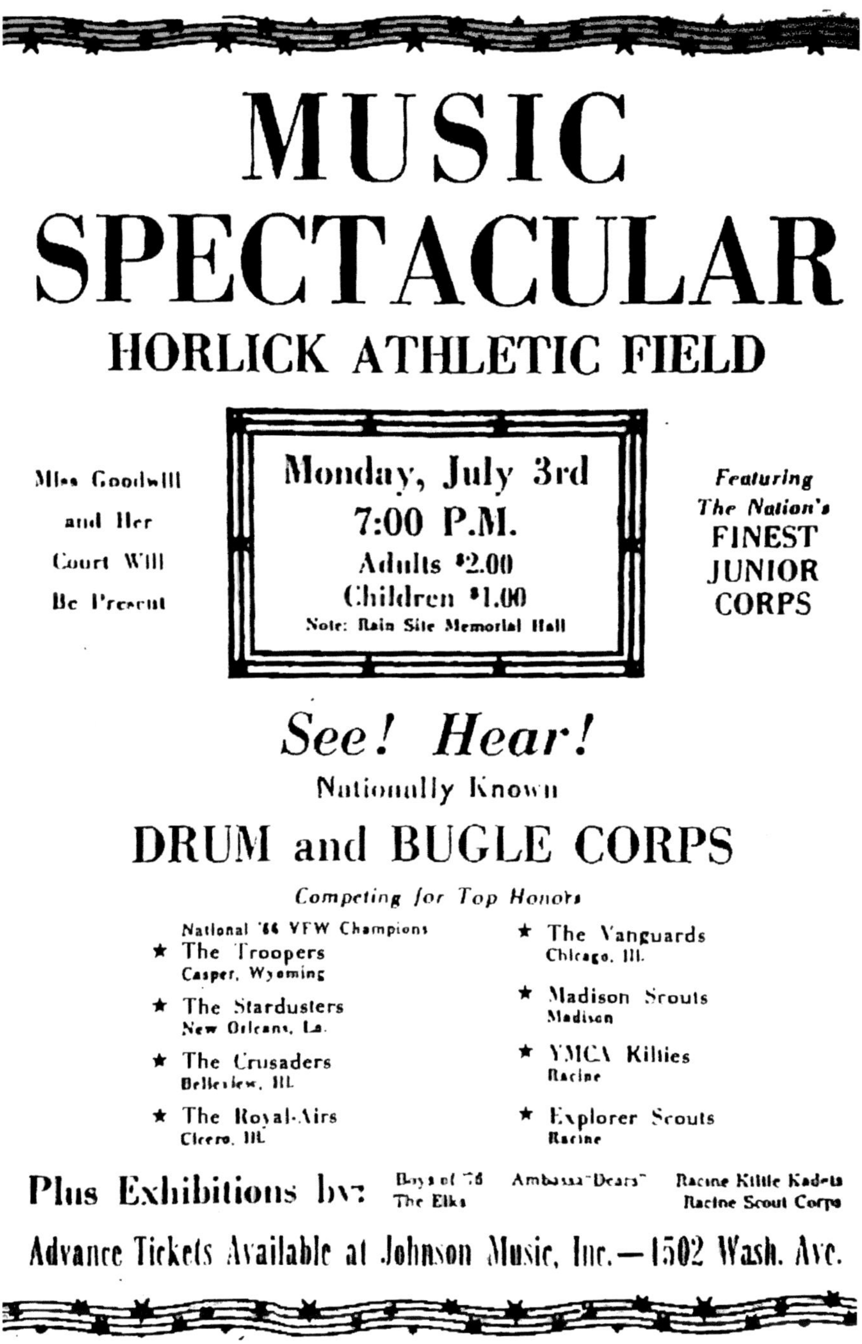
MUSIC
SPECTACULAR
HORLICK ATHLETIC FIELD
Miss Goodwill and Her Court Will Be Present
Monday, July 3rd
7:00 P.M.
Adults $2.00
Children $1.00
Note: Rain Site Memorial Hall
Featuring The Nation's FINEST JUNIOR CORPS
See! Hear!
Nationally Known
DRUM and BUGLE CORPS
Competing for Top Honors
National '66 VFW Champions
★ The Troopers
Casper, Wyoming
★ The Stardusters
New Orleans, La.
★ The Crusaders
Belleview, Ill.
★ The Royal-Airs
Cicero, Ill.
★ The Vanguards
Chicago, Ill.
★ Madison Scouts
Madison
★ YMCA Kilties
Racine
★ Explorer Scouts
Racine
Plus Exhibitions by:
Boys of '76
The Elks
Ambassa-"Dears"
Racine Kiltie Kadets
Racine Scout Corps
Advance Tickets Available at Johnson Music, Inc.—1502 Wash. Ave.

1962 and 1968, only one corps beat the Racine Scouts at VFW prelims but did not make finals). Corps that didn't beat the Racine Scouts in prelims usually didn't make finals. At the time of this show, the Racine Scouts had not beaten any of Chicago's big three or the Troopers in three years. And all four were in this show.

The Racine Scouts was good in 1966 and better in 1967, but no one expected it to win this show. Only the members of the Racine Scouts felt that they had a chance. But the corps put on one of those magical Horlick Field performances, perhaps the best in the corps' long history, got a wild reaction from the packed house and won the show.

People continue to argue whether it was a deserved victory or some sort of conspiracy. But to this day, it remains the only drum corps contest that the Racine Scouts ever won in Horlick Field.

JULY 3, 1967—GOODWILL SPECTACULAR

1. 73.500 Racine Scouts....................................V6
2. 73.166 Royal Airs...V4
3. 72.733 Des Plaines Vanguard V3
4. 71.666 Troopers..V2
5. 65.466 Belleville Crusaders (Millstadt Crusaders) ... V8
6. 64.733 Kilties V5
7. 52.566 Stardusters
8. 46.266 Madison Scouts

Exhibition

Boys of '76
AmbassaDears
Racine Junior Scouts
Kiltie Kadets

Scout Corps Takes 3rd 1st in 3 Days
The Racine Explorer Scouts Drum and Bugle Corps grabbed first place honors for the third time in three consecutive days Monday night. Edging out the Chicago Royal Airs by less than four-tenths of a point, the Explorers topped seven other corps in the Goodwill Spectacular junior drum and bugle corps competition at Horlick Athletic Field. Judges gave the Explorers 73.5 points to 73.166 for the Royal Airs.

The host unit for the show, the Boys of '76, was honored during the activities by becoming the third senior corps to be admitted to the Drum Corps Hall of Fame. The Boys of '76, founded in 1926, is the oldest

American Legion drum corps in the nation still in existence. The unit has been national champion four times.

Third place in Monday night's competition went to the Skokie, Ill, Vanguards with last year's Veterans of Foreign Wars champion, the Casper, Wyo. Troopers, finishing fourth. The Belleville, Ill. Crusaders placed fifth; Racine YMCA Kilties, sixth; New Orleans Stardusters, seventh and Madison Explorer Scouts, eighth.

—Racine Journal Times, *July 5, 1967*

A Racine Scout Memory

The lineup of corps for the show was the strongest since the East-West Spectacular in 1964. Of all the corps slated to appear, the only corps that we had never beaten during my tenure as a Racine Scout was the Royal Airs.

I think that our 1967 corps was the best in all the years that I marched. We had won two shows in a row and, as we performed our show, we got a good crowd response. We weren't used to that in Racine. In fact we were considered the third favorite hometown corps, the first two being the Troopers and the Kilties in that order. The Troopers always got the largest crowd response. When our show was done, we felt pretty good about our performance. The staff herded the corps to the very dark southwest corner of Horlick Field behind the west grandstand and they told us that it was the worst performance of that year and that we were simply awful and should be embarrassed. They ripped us for over ten minutes. It took the wind out of our sails. As I made my way towards the stands after being yelled at, a few Cavaliers that I knew told me that it was the best performance they had ever seen from us. I was more than a bit perplexed, but we believed our staff and thought we were going to lose to everybody.

During the finale when we heard "in sixth place from Racine, Wisconsin," we braced ourselves for the inevitable. My immediate feeling was that we just got beat by the Millstadt Crusaders for the first time ever, but the announcer said "the Kilties!" As the announcing of scores and places progressed, we thought it possible that they forgot that we were in the show as our score was not announced. When the Royal Airs were announced in second place, our jaws dropped. It was quite a surprise to say the least, after how badly our staff had ripped us.

In those years, finales or retreats were still held with the full corps on the field for the announcing of scores and the corps exited in reverse order of the

The Chicago Royal Airs, 1967. The Royal Airs performed in Horlick Field five times between 1962 and 1968 and took second each time. *Courtesy of Moe Knox.*

> *scores playing as they passed the winner in review. The last corps to pass in front of us was the Royal Airs. As they played "Of Thee I Sing," the soloist, who shall remain nameless (and I consider him to be a great friend to this day) didn't play his usual solo. Instead, he turned towards us and played taps. His corps director was said to have had words with him after.*
> *—Mike Kaufman, Racine Scouts, 1967*

August 5—Music on the March

This was a lesser upset and not really an upset when examined. LaSalle Cadets had narrowly beaten the Racine Scouts earlier in Canada, and the Scouts had beaten the Kilties by nine points in Horlick Field a month earlier.

But expectations at the time were that few, if any, Canadian corps could beat a decent U.S. corps. LaSalle dispelled that notion in 1967. LaSalle Cadets had a crisp, loud, fast style that was unusual in the Midwest, and the crowd loved the corps. LaSalle beat the Kilties by over a point to win in its first appearance in Horlick Field.

The show had thirteen corps with three finalists and the Canadian corps that beat them all.

August 5, 1967—Music on the March

Class A

1. 77.2 LaSalle Cadets
2. 75.9 Kilties V5
3. 73.0 Blue Stars V10
4. 60.1 Madison Scouts
5. 59.9 Fort Dodge Lancers
5. 59.9 Northernaires

Class C

1. 57.2 AmbassaDears
2. 56.6 St. Matthias Preps
3. 45.1 Kiltie Kadets
4. 44.9 Madison Junior Scouts
5. 42.3 Racine Junior Scouts

Exhibition

Racine Scouts V6
Boys of '76

Chapter 10

West Coast Drum and Bugle Corps Arrive

1968

1968 Statistics

Number of shows 2
Drum corps performances 24
States represented 7
VFW champion performances 2
Championship finalist performances 13

The year 1968 was when the West Coast arrived in Horlick Field: both the Buena Vista, California Velvet Knights and the Sentinels of Bellevue, Washington, appeared. In all, corps came from six states and Canada. The Troopers appeared twice.

Kilties, 1968. *Courtesy of Moe Knox.*

Both shows were exceptional. The first had four of the top five drum corps at the 1968 VFW nationals and six finalists overall. The second had three of the top four drum corps and seven finalists overall.

The senior Boys of '76 competed against junior corps during these years. There weren't many seniors to compete against anymore. The Kilties took only third and fourth place in the two Horlick Field contests in 1968 but went on to win the 1968 VFW and World Open championships.

JULY 3—GOODWILL SPECTACULAR

This show could be called a mini-nationals. It had the top three drum and bugle corps from the 1968 VFW nationals competition and four of the top five.

The year 1968 was, like 1966, very competitive. At VFW nationals prelims, the top five corps were within 0.9 of a point. At finals, they were separated by only 1.9 points. At the 1968 Goodwill Spectacular, the eventual national champion Racine Kilties took fourth. The Royal Airs beat the Cavaliers by two points in this show yet lost to them at nationals. In competitive years like this, performances were usually thrilling because each corps was fighting to win and any of them might. Oddly, for the second year in a row, Royal Airs took second place at the Goodwill Spectacular with the identical score of 73.166.

JULY 3, 1968—GOODWILL SPECTACULAR
1. 74.600 Troopers...V3
2. 73.166 Royal Airs..V5
3. 71.133 Cavaliers...V2
4. 68.800 Kilties...V1
5. 57.766 Racine Scouts...V9
6. 52.766 Kenosha Queensmen
7. 48.733 Stardusters..A3
8. 46.300 Mariners

Exhibition
Boys of '76
AmbassaDears
Racine Junior Scouts
Kiltie Kadets

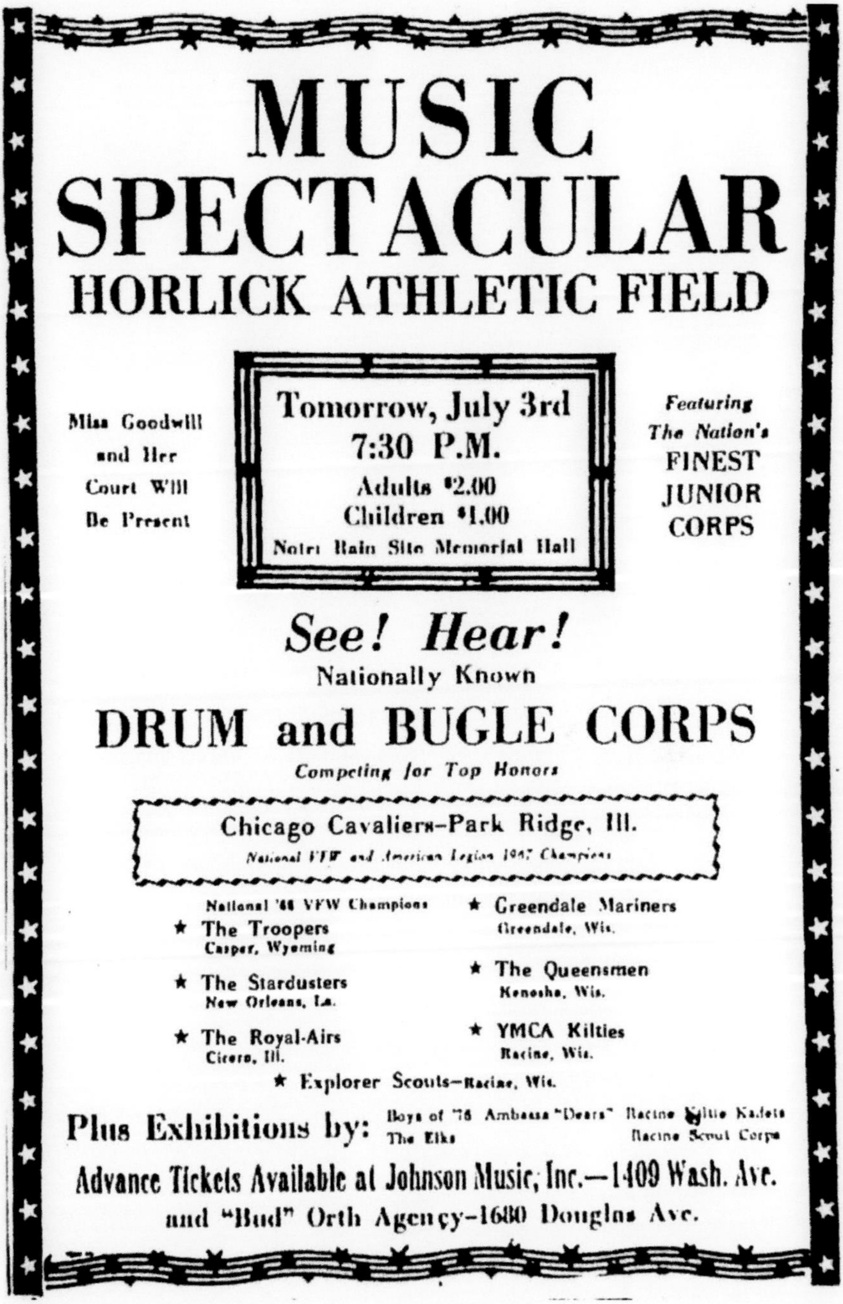
MUSIC SPECTACULAR
HORLICK ATHLETIC FIELD
Miss Goodwill and Her Court Will Be Present
Tomorrow, July 3rd
7:30 P.M.
Adults $2.00
Children $1.00
Notre Rain Site Memorial Hall
Featuring The Nation's FINEST JUNIOR CORPS
See! Hear!
Nationally Known
DRUM and BUGLE CORPS
Competing for Top Honors
Chicago Cavaliers–Park Ridge, Ill.
★ The Troopers
Casper, Wyoming
★ The Stardusters
New Orleans, La.
★ The Royal-Airs
Cicero, Ill.
★ Greendale Mariners
Greendale, Wis.
★ The Queensmen
Kenosha, Wis.
★ YMCA Kilties
Racine, Wis.
★ Explorer Scouts–Racine, Wis.
Plus Exhibitions by:
Boys of '76
Ambassa "Dears"
The Elks
Racine Scout Corps
Advance Tickets Available at Johnson Music, Inc.—1409 Wash. Ave.
and "Bud" Orth Agency–1680 Douglas Ave.

The Stardusters from Metairie, Louisiana, 1968. *Courtesy of Moe Knox.*

AUGUST 10—MUSIC ON THE MARCH

Drum Corps from Canada to California Vie Aug. 10
Drum corps from California and Canada will be among nine corps competing Saturday night, Aug. 10, at Racine's annual "Music on the March." The show is sponsored by the Racine Scout Corps Parents' Club and will include an exhibition by the Racine Explorer Scouts Drum and Bugle Corps while judges tally totals for the competing corps.

Starts at 6:45 p.m.
The show at Horlick Athletic Field gets underway at 6:45 p.m. with the Racine Elks Youth Band conducting a flag raising ceremony and then presenting a field exhibition. The California entry is the Velvet Knights of Buena Park, making its first Midwest appearance. Music arranger for the corps is Jack Sterns, Hollywood television music arranger who has produced music for such personalities as Bing Crosby and Rosemary Clooney.

The Canadian corps is the defending champion LaSalle Cadets of Ottawa. Other entrants: The Casper, Wyo. Troopers, which placed first in the July 3rd Goodwill Spectacular and is seeking its second win in two appearances in Racine; Madison Scout Senior Corps, which will be first off the line in the field competition at about 7 p.m.; The Vanguards, one of

PRESENTING OUR ANNUAL
DRUM CORPS EXTRAVAGANZA
"MUSIC ON THE MARCH"
SATURDAY, AUG. 10, 7 P.M. • HORLICK FIELD
CLASS A CORPS IN FIELD COMPETITION
• VELVET KNIGHTS (California)
• VANGUARDS (Des Plaines, Ill.)
• IMPERIALS (Norwood Park, Ill.)
• TROOPERS (Casper, Wyoming)
• LaSALLE CADETS (Ottawa, Ont.)
• RACINE KILTIES
• MADISON SCOUTS
• FIRST FEDERAL BLUE STARS (La Crosse)
• RACINE BOYS OF '76
EXHIBITIONS BY . . .
• RACINE JUNIOR SCOUTS
• RACINE EXPLORER SCOUTS
• ELKS YOUTH BAND
Come and Enjoy an Evening With These Top Units From Many States and Canada
Presented by
RACINE SCOUT CORPS PARENTS CLUB
ADMISSION
This ad Sponsored as a Community Service by
WEST RACINE BUSINESS & PROFESSIONAL MEN'S ASSOCIATION

> *two Illinois corps entered in the show; The Norwood Park, Ill., Imperials, which will take the field with 39 horns, 16 drums and a 24-girl color guard;…Racine's American Legion "Boys of '76" which is entered as a competing corps in the open class show; The YMCA Kilties of Racine; Federal Blue Stars of La Crosse. Order of appearance for the competing corps will be Madison, La Crosse, Velvet Knights, Boys of '76, Imperials, Kilties, Troopers, Vanguards, and LaSalle Cadets.*
>
> *The sponsors announced they have contracted to have Horlick Field sprayed on Saturday for mosquito control.*
>
> —Racine Journal Times, *August 8, 1968*

This may have been the best Scout show ever. It was a mirror image of the first 1968 show, with five of the same units and similar, though not quite as good, quality of units as the Spectacular show. It had the VFW national champion, three of the top four VFW finalist units and seven championship show finalists.

It also hosted two West Coast drum corps, the Velvet Knights and the Sentinels. As with the Troopers five years earlier, the audience expected little of them. At every nationals, West Coast corps had fared poorly against eastern and midwestern corps. But the corps were from the West Coast, and that alone was a draw. None had ever appeared in the Midwest before. Everyone was curious to see what a West Coast corps was like. Neither drum corps made the impact that the Troopers had. Velvet Knights finished seventh, twenty-three points behind the winning corps, while the Sentinels finished ninth, twenty-eight points back.

August 10, 1968—Music on the March

1. 79.65 Des Plaines Vanguard V4
2. 78.30 Troopers V3
3. 77.73 Kilties V1
4. 73.12 Blue Stars V8
5. 67.82 Norwood Park Imperials V12
6. 67.38 LaSalle Cadets
7. 56.85 Velvet Knights
8. 53.88 Madison Scouts
9. 52.03 Boys of '76 .... A2
10. 51.25 Sentinels

Exhibition

Racine Junior Scouts

Racine Scouts V9

Des Plaines Vanguard, 1968. *Courtesy of Moe Knox.*

The Des Plaines Vanguard, which won this and a lot of shows in 1968, was an extremely large and loud drum and bugle corps for 1968. It had absorbed members from many Chicago-area corps that had folded in the years 1965–67, including Custer's Brigade, St. Andrew's Hornets, Morton Grove Spartans, Morton Grove Cougars, St. Michael's Chi-Angels and Jackson Raiders. The 1968 Vanguard had an amazing thirty-four flags. In comparison, in that year, the only other major corps with twenty or more flags were the Troopers with twenty-four and the Racine Scouts with twenty. Most corps had just ten to sixteen. The Vanguard won this show by over a point. The corps took first at World Open prelims and finals and first at VFW prelims. But in this very competitive year, it fell to fourth at VFW finals, 1.6 behind the champion Kilties. The Vanguard first appeared in Horlick Field in 1952 as Mel Tierney and appeared a total of ten times.

Chapter 11

The Must-Play Place

1969–1978

In 1962, few drum and bugle corps toured. By 1968, dozens of very good drum and bugle corps were making at least one extended tour outside their region each season. Between 1969 and 1978, the drum corps activity boomed, and scores of big, entertaining corps took extended and often multiple tours each year.

Horlick Field was a must-play place for these touring corps. The stories had been around for years: big, enthusiastic crowds, good pay and tough competition from a lot of different regions. Corps came to make their own stories.

In the ten seasons from 1969 through 1978, Horlick Field hosted 38 drum and bugle corps shows with 319* individual drum corps performances, an average of almost 4 shows and 32 performances a year. Over the same period, Horlick Field hosted 93 championship finalist performances—9 per year—and one of the year's national champions 12 times.

*The list of corps that performed in one show was not found, and many exhibition performances were not recorded, or this number would be much higher.

Chapter 12

FOUR SHOWS, FORTY-FOUR PERFORMANCES, FOUR CALIFORNIA CORPS, FOUR PERFORMANCES BY NATIONAL CHAMPIONS

1969

1969 STATISTICS

Number of shows 4
Drum corps performances 44
States represented 6
VFW champion performances 3
American Legion champion performances..... 1
Championship finalist performances 16

The year 1969 was like 1968 doubled. Four shows, forty-four corps performances, sixteen finalists, four performances by a national champion. One contest had the top three VFW corps of the year and two corps from California. A second contest had the VFW champion, seven finalists, two different California corps and units from New York and Massachusetts. A third contest had the national champion and three other finalists.

The Velvet Knights came for the second year and was joined by the Princemen from Pinole, California; the Anaheim Kingsmen; and the Santa Clara Vanguard. For the second straight year, the Troopers appeared twice.

May 31—Kiltie Kadet Show

The season opened with the Kiltie Kadets Class B show on May 31. Of the nine drum and bugle corps in the contest, three were all-girl and two were all-boy; two were from Iowa and one was from Illinois. This was the tenth appearance in Horlick Field by the Mercury Thunderbolts and its first and only win. Mercy High School All-girl drum corps from Milwaukee, which had first appeared in 1952, made its third and last appearance in Horlick Field at this show.

May 31, 1969—Kiltie Kadet Show
Class B
1. 61.5 Mercury Thunderbolts
2. 57.9 Mercy High School All-girl
3. 56.2 Colt 45s
4. 53.1 Guardsmen
5. 38.8 Nee-Hi's
6. 31.0 St. Brendan's Patriots
7. 30.4 AmbassaDears
8. 22.8 Racine Junior Scouts

Exhibition
Kiltie Kadets

July 3—Goodwill Spectacular

Thursday, Racine's Kilties and Explorers will be competing with six other leading corps from across the nation for top honors and a $600 prize in the Goodwill Spectacular. Second prize is $450. The remainder of the $2,000 in prize money ranges from $325 third-place award, to $75 for seventh and eight places…

Troopers to Compete
Chief rival of the two Racine corps will be the 1968 North American Invitational and C.Y.O champion Troopers, from Casper, Wyo. Also in the competition will be two corps from California, one from Illinois, and one from both Milwaukee and Kenosha. Judging will be done by representatives from the Central States Judges Association. The drum corps spectacular will also

1969 GOODWILL SPECTACULAR

HORLICK ATHLETIC FIELD

Miss Goodwill and Her Court Will Be Present

Thursday, July 3rd
7:30 P.M.
Adults $2.00
Children $1.00
Note: Rain Site Memorial Hall

Featuring The Nation's FINEST JUNIOR CORPS

See! Hear!

Nationally Known

DRUM and BUGLE CORPS

Competing for Top Honors

The Troopers – Casper, Wyoming
1968 North American Invitational and CYO Champions

- ★ Racine Kilties
  1968 VFW Champions
- ★ Velvet Knights
  Buena Park, Calif.
- ★ Chicago Cavaliers
  Park Ridge, Illinois
- ★ The Queensmen
  Kenosha, Wis.
- ★ The Princemen
  San Mateo, Calif.
- ★ St. Patrick Imperials
  Milwaukee, Wis.
- ★ Explorer Scouts Racine, Wis

Plus Exhibitions by: Boys of '76 Ambassa "Dears" Racine Kiltie Kadets The Elks Racine Scout Corps

Advance Tickets Available at

Johnson Music, Inc., 1409 Wash. Ave. – King Ehrlich, 4101 Wash. Ave. – Guy Lloyd, 1644 Wash. Ave. – Charles Realty, 1235 Douglas Ave.

> *include exhibitions by the Boys of '76, Ambassa "Dears," Kiltie Kadets, and the Racine Scout drum and bugle corps, and the Elks Youth Band.*
> —Racine Journal Times, *July 2, 1969*

This was the fourth time in seven years—and second time in two years—that Horlick Field hosted the top three VFW drum and bugle corps of the year in one show, and they finished in this show in the same order that they would finish at nationals: Kilties first, Cavaliers second and Troopers third. This show also had the distinction of hosting both the VFW national champion and the American Legion national champion in a head-to-head contest.

July 3, 1969—Goodwill Spectacular

1. 78.95 Kilties V1
2. 77.05 Cavaliers V2 A1
3. 74.75 Troopers V3 A2
4. 65.90 Velvet Knights
5. 65.40 Racine Scouts A8
6. 54.60 St. Patrick's Imperials
7. 53.10 Kenosha Queensmen
8. 44.35 Princemen

Exhibition

Boys of '76 .... A4
AmbassaDears
Racine Junior Scouts
Kiltie Kadets

The Horlick Field crowd was so entirely taken with the "hometown" Troopers by this time that when the corps was announced in third place, the crowd booed lustily. It still annoys some members of the Kilties. They were defending VFW national champion and on their way to their second straight national title, and their hometown crowd booed when they beat the Troopers.

August 9—Music on the March

A month after hosting the top three corps of the year, Horlick Field hosted another great show with the first- and third-best VFW corps and seven

PRESENTING OUR ANNUAL
DRUM CORPS EXTRAVAGANZA
"MUSIC ON THE MARCH"
SATURDAY, AUGUST 9 • HORLICK FIELD
CLASS "C" CORPS – 5:45 P.M.
• QUEENSMAN SQUIRES (Kenosha) • KILTIE KADETS
• BOY SCOUT CORPS
OPEN CLASS COMPETITION – 7:30 P.M.
• VANGUARDS (Des Plaines, Ill.)
• TROOPERS (Casper, Wyoming)
• RACINE KILTIES
• ST. RITA'S BRASSMEN (Brooklyn)
• RACINE BOYS OF '76
• ST. FRANCIS XAVIER (S. Weymouth, Mass.)
• KINGSMEN (Anaheim, Calif.)
• VANGUARDS (Santa Clara, Calif.)
• BLUE STARS (La Crosse)
• QUEENSMEN (Kenosha)
• BOSTON CRUSADERS (Boston, Mass.)
EXHIBITIONS BY . . .
• RACINE AMBASSA"DEARS" • RACINE EXPLORER SCOUTS
• ELKS YOUTH BAND
Come and Enjoy an Evening With These
Top Units From Many States
PRESENTED BY
RACINE SCOUT CORPS
PARENTS CLUB
Entire area will be sprayed for mosquito control prior to the competition.
In case of rain, competition will be moved to Horlick Field House.
Admission
Advance Tickets $2.00 (Call 633-4465 or 639-1558)
At the Gate: $2.50 • Children Under 12: 75c

finalists overall. It had two corps from California; one each from Wyoming, New York and Massachusetts; and two corps named the Vanguard. Overall, it had fifteen drum and bugle corps and was the third-largest show in Horlick Field history.

During this summer, when Des Plaines was announced as the Vanguard, people in the audience often shouted, "The real Vanguard!" But the Santa Clara Vanguard was only four points behind the "real Vanguard" at this show and was on the rise. The next year would be different.

The Horlick Field crowd was happier this time: the Troopers beat the Kilties.

AUGUST 9, 1969—MUSIC ON THE MARCH

1. 73.55 Troopers..V3 A2
2. 70.40 Kilties..V1
3. 68.75 Anaheim Kingsmen.......................................V9 A4

Troopers, 1969. The Troopers performed in Horlick Field twice each in 1968, 1969 and 1970. *Photo by Paul Stott from the collection of* Drum Corps World.

4. 67.05 Des Plaines Vanguard V6
5. 66.55 Blue Stars V7
6. 64.50 St. Rita's Brassmen
7. 63.30 Santa Clara Vanguard
8. 62.55 Boys of '76 .... A4
9. 48.30 Kenosha Queensmen
10. 44.45 St. Francis Sancians

Class C

1. 60.225 Kiltie Kadets
2. 57.775 Racine Junior Scouts
3. 57.425 Kenosha Squires

Exhibition

Racine Scouts.. A8
AmbassaDears

August 30—Labor Day Drums

This late-season show was held after VFW nationals, and as in all such shows, all of the corps were short a number of performers who had gone back to school. It had eight corps and four finalists. The *Racine Journal Times* reported that six thousand people were in the audience.

The Blue Stars, 1969. The Blue Stars appeared twice in Horlick Field in 1969 and sixteen times overall. *Courtesy of Moe Knox.*

AUGUST 30, 1969—LABOR DAY DRUMS

1. 73.60 Blue Stars V7
2. 70.05 Madison Scouts
3. 68.30 Racine Scouts.. A8
4. 59.60 Mariners
5. 58.10 Kenosha Queensmen
6. 56.40 Boys of '76 .... A4

Exhibition

Kilties V1
AmbassaDears

The Blue Stars was formed in 1964, performed in 1965 as a parade corps, entered competition in 1966, first made VFW finals in 1967 and took second at the first DCI championship contest in 1972. The first thing that people might recall about the early years of the Blue Stars were the very short shorts of the very large color guard. But by 1972, the Blue Stars was an annual contender. It was one of the key drum corps of the first years of DCI.

Chapter 13

THREE PERFORMANCES BY NATIONAL CHAMPIONS

1970

1970 Statistics

Number of shows.. 4
Drum corps performances............................36
States represented 7
VFW champion performances........................ 2
American Legion champion performances..... 1
Championship finalist performances 13

The year 1970 was the fifth time in eight years that Horlick Field hosted at least three drum and bugle corps shows. It was also the third year in a row in which Horlick Field hosted the VFW national championship drum and bugle corps at least twice. In 1968 and 1969, it was the hometown Kilties. In 1970, the adopted-hometown VFW national champion Troopers appeared twice and the American Legion national champion Santa Clara Vanguard appeared once.

A Class B show opened the year and then two remarkable Class A shows followed. Both had the national champion and a total of four finalists. One of the shows had both the American Legion and VFW national champions going head to head. At a time when West Coast corps were still rare, both shows had one California corps, and one of the shows had two California corps and one from New York. The Troopers, Kilties, Racine Scouts and Blue Stars were in both Class A shows.

At the end of 1969, Dave Richards had taken over the horn line of the Boys of '76, become drum major and recruited many former members of the Racine Scouts, St. Patrick's Imperials and Kenosha Queensmen to join. Filled with new, young talent, Boys of '76 went to DCA championships in 1970 and became the first Midwest Senior corps to ever make Drum Corps Associates (DCA) finals, placing seventh in prelims and ninth in finals. But without any senior competition in the Midwest, Boys of '76 competed against junior corps all summer.

May 31—Kiltie Kadet Show

While this Class B show had the sixth-place finisher at the American Legion championships of 1970 in the Americanos, few corps went to American Legion nationals in 1970. The Americanos fell to Guardsmen and the Oshkosh Warriors in this show. The Warriors was a good, entertaining unit from central Wisconsin that folded after the 1972 season.

May 31, 1970—Kiltie Kadet Show
Class B
1. 74.00 Oshkosh Warriors
2. 72.85 Guardsmen
3. 72.35 Americanos A6
4. 60.03 Crusader-Gladiators
5. 48.85 Militaires

July 3—Goodwill Spectacular

For the second year in a row, the Goodwill Spectacular hosted the year's VFW and American Legion national champions in one show. While the show hosted corps from only three states, one of those states was California and another Wyoming, and both corps were national champions in 1970. Overall, it had eleven corps and five championship show finalists.

July 3, 1970—Goodwill Spectacular
1. 76.00 Troopers V1
2. 73.10 Santa Clara Vanguard A1
3. 72.50 Blue Stars V5

4. 69.10 Kilties V6
5. 53.65 Mercury Thunderbolts
6. 51.10 Racine Scouts
7. 45.65 St. Patrick's Imperials

Exhibition

Boys of '76 .... DCA9
Racine Junior Scouts
AmbassaDears
Kiltie Kadets

A Santa Clara Vanguard Memory

The night Santa Clara became the *Vanguard*
The year was 1970 and our first show in the Midwest just happened to be in Racine. Ya know Racine, in the heart of drum corps land. Home to the two time defending champions Kilties as well as the Racine Scouts. Now we weren't all that bad. After all the corps just missed finals in 1969 by .05 and we did just defeat the Kingsmen to become California State Champs, but this was the big time.

Here I was in my first big show and I felt so inferior in my red and green satin top with black pants. I mean we were standing in the same area as the Kilties and the Troopers. The Kilts looked so much older and bigger than us and the Troopers in those 7th Cavalry uniforms looked so cool. To top it off the stands were packed with fans that were used to seeing the best that drum corps had to offer.

Finally it was time to perform. About twelve measures into the off the line something amazing happened. The fans started to rise in a standing ovation. They stayed standing until we stopped for our concert. Fred Sanchez started concert with his bari solo. By the time Wayne Downey came out for his sop solo the stands had already erupted into another enthusiastic standing ovation. As we finished our concert I couldn't believe the crowd's reaction, they were going crazy. After they settled down, our DM called out "Resume Hut" and we were off with "Richman" and once again the crowd went crazy. After we finished our show and snapped our horns down we were greeted by the PA announcer screaming over the crowd "Wonderful show!... Wonderful show!... The Santa Clara Vanguard!"

We didn't win that night. We lost to the Troopers by a penalty. Gale Royer stated that the crowd got us so pumped, that we marched the whole

The Santa Clara Vanguard, 1970. *From the collection of* Drum Corps World.

> *second half of the show at almost double time and the show ended up over a minute short.*
>
> *What an amazing night! We basically received a standing ovation from start to finish. In my four years in the corps nothing compared to the excitement of that night.*
>
> *—Paul C. Towne, Santa Clara Vanguard, 1970*

The famed Drum Corps International (DCI) champion and longtime powerhouse Santa Clara Vanguard drum and bugle corps came of age at Horlick Field on July 3, 1970. In 1969, the corps finished out of finals in thirteenth place, and little was expected of them in 1970. At the time, California corps were still considered novelties. The 1970 Spectacular changed the minds of the drum corps community and of the corps itself. The corps' turbocharged performance and the thunderous, frenzied reaction by the Horlick Field audience defined the Santa Clara Vanguard as a new national power.

Santa Clara would likely have been in the top six at VFW finals in 1970, but the corps did not make the long trip to Miami. Instead, it won the 1970 American Legion national championship in Portland by 4.0 points over the Anaheim Kingsmen. In 1971, the corps won the VFW national championship by a point over the defending champion Troopers. In 1972, it was heavily favored to win the first DCI championship (it won preliminaries by 2.4 points, an amazing spread at a national preliminaries contest in any year) but took third at finals in a shocking upset. It won the DCI championship in 1973, 1974, 1978, 1981, 1989 and 1999. It is the only corps to make every single DCI finals competition.

And it all began on July 3, 1970, in Horlick Athletic Field.

AUGUST 8—MUSIC ON THE MARCH

The Racine Scouts' annual show had one drum and bugle corps from Wyoming, two from California and one from New York. It was Anaheim Kingsmen's second and Velvet Knights' third appearance in Horlick Field in three years. And it was Blue Stars' fifth time in Horlick Field between 1968 and 1970. Overall, the contest had eleven drum corps from five states; five of the corps were finalists.

AUGUST 8, 1970—MUSIC ON THE MARCH

1. 82.90 Troopers V1
2. 79.70 Blue Stars V5
3. 78.30 Kilties V6
4. 74.35 Anaheim Kingsmen A2
5. 72.60 St. Paul Scouts
6. 70.65 Des Plaines Vanguard
7. 69.50 Velvet Knights A3
8. 39.70 Kingston Indians
9. 31.80 32nd Hussars

Exhibition

Racine Scouts
Racine Junior Scouts

September 5—Labor Day Spectacle

Only one out-of-state corps appeared in this show held after VFW nationals. Six of the nine corps in the show were based fewer than 25 miles from Horlick Field. The Waterloo Royals came over 250 miles for its first appearance in Horlick Field.

The Mariners was a big, colorful and entertaining corps that was years ahead of the activity in showmanship. One year, the corps shot off fireworks from its flagpoles. Other corps complained that the Mariners show was filled with "cheap drum corps tricks," but audiences loved them. Surprisingly, though based only ten miles away, the Mariners appeared in Horlick Field only nine times.

September 5, 1970—Labor Day Spectacle

1. 78.2 Madison Scouts..V7
2. 68.5 Mercury Thunderbolts
3. 65.2 Racine Scouts
4. 63.3 St. Patrick's Imperials
5. 56.8 Royals
6. 55.8 Mariners

Exhibition

Kilties...V6
Kiltie Kadets
AmbassaDears

Chapter 14

Anaheim Kingsmen Wins by Ten

1971

1971 Statistics

Number of shows.. 2
Drum corps performances........................... 23
States represented 8
Championship finalist performances 3

After hosting four shows in both 1969 and 1970, Horlick Field hosted only two shows in 1971. It saw only three appearances by a VFW national championship finalist. However, the contests again showed great variety, with drum and bugle corps from eight states and three coasts. The Anaheim Kingsmen, the best corps to appear all year, won the Goodwill Spectacular by ten points and placed fifth at the last VFW nationals before it was superseded by the first DCI championship contest in 1972.

July 3—Goodwill Spectacular

This show was not the typical top-quality Horlick Field show; it had only one VFW national championship finalist. But it was an example of the other defining characteristic of Horlick Field drum and bugle corps shows: it had great variety. It had drum corps from six states, including Washington, California, Kansas and Louisiana. It had two all-boy corps, one all-girl corps and an all-black corps.

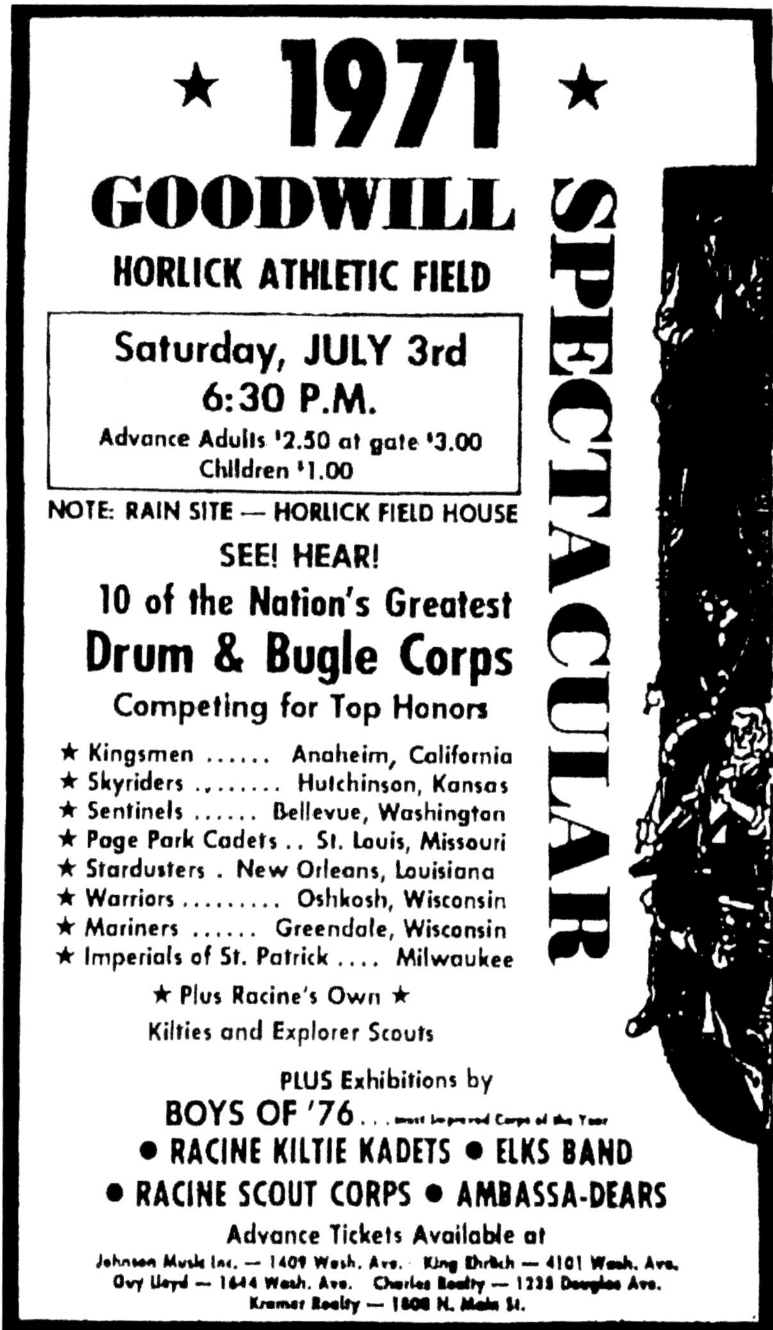
★ 1971 ★
GOODWILL
SPECTACULAR
HORLICK ATHLETIC FIELD
Saturday, JULY 3rd
6:30 P.M.
Advance Adults '2.50 at gate '3.00
Children '1.00
NOTE: RAIN SITE — HORLICK FIELD HOUSE
SEE! HEAR!
10 of the Nation's Greatest
Drum & Bugle Corps
Competing for Top Honors
★ Kingsmen ...... Anaheim, California
★ Skyriders .... Hutchinson, Kansas
★ Sentinels ...... Bellevue, Washington
★ Page Park Cadets .. St. Louis, Missouri
★ Stardusters . New Orleans, Louisiana
★ Warriors .... Oshkosh, Wisconsin
★ Mariners ...... Greendale, Wisconsin
★ Imperials of St. Patrick .... Milwaukee
★ Plus Racine's Own ★
Kilties and Explorer Scouts
PLUS Exhibitions by
BOYS OF '76 ...
• RACINE KILTIE KADETS • ELKS BAND
• RACINE SCOUT CORPS • AMBASSA-DEARS
Advance Tickets Available at

July 3, 1971—Goodwill Spectacular

1. 81.90 Anaheim Kingsmen V5
2. 71.90 Sky Ryders
3. 71.45 Kilties
4. 70.85 Stardusters.. A3
5. 69.50 St. Patrick's Imperials
6. 66.85 Racine Scouts
7. 63.85 Oshkosh Warriors
8. 56.70 Page Park Cadets
9. 56.30 Mariners
10. 51.25 Sentinels

Exhibition

Boys of '76
Kiltie Kadets
Racine Junior Scouts
AmbassaDears

In the picture below, the AmbassaDears are on the field while the Kiltie Kadets stand on the starting line at the 1971 Goodwill Spectacular. This was only the preshow exhibition of a not particularly good show, but there are already over seven thousand people in the grandstands, end zone to end zone.

Horlick Field, July 3, 1971. Racine Journal Times, *July 5, 1971.*

August 7—Music on the March

The two best corps at the Racine Scouts' show were the Kilties and St. Paul Scouts, and the latter took eleventh at a VFW nationals to which few of the top corps went. The Kilties, one of the many corps that did not go, would likely have made finals. The show had nine corps from five states and both coasts, so it offered the audience a wide variety of regional styles in a time when there were still regional differences.

The Boys of '76 competed against junior corps during this period, as there were few, if any, midwestern senior competitions.

August 7, 1971—Music on the March

1. 79.40 Kilties
2. 73.65 St. Paul Scouts..V11
3. 65.85 Long Island Kingsmen
4. 64.00 Seattle Imperials
5. 61.85 Mariners
6. 59.05 Boys of '76
7. 48.35 Trailblazers

Exhibition

Racine Scouts
Racine Junior Scouts

Chapter 15

The Best Show in Horlick Athletic Field History

1972

1972 Statistics

Number of shows 3
Drum corps performances 32
States represented 9
DCA champion performances 1
Championship finalist performances 11

The year 1972 was a special one and arguably the best example of the unique, wonderful synergy of drum and bugle corps, the close confines of Horlick Athletic Field and its knowledgeable audience.

The first two shows were middling shows for Horlick Field. The first had two DCI finalists and an all-girl corps from Canada. The second had only two out-of-state corps. But the third show was magical.

July 3—Goodwill Spectacular

This was the first of only two performances in Horlick Field by the Belleville Black Knights, a longtime Midwest powerhouse from Illinois near St. Louis. The corps finished as high as second at VFW in 1959 and tenth at DCI in 1973. This was the first of two performances in Horlick Field in 1972 by the St. Paul Scouts. The show had two all-girl corps, five all-male corps and corps from four states and Canada.

The newspaper ad for the show proclaimed, "800 Bodies in the show—Where else but the Drum Corps Capital of the World."

July 3, 1972—Goodwill Spectacular
1. 78.25 Des Plaines Vanguard D7
2. 78.10 Kilties D8
3. 72.25 Belleville Black Knights
4. 69.70 Racine Scouts
5. 69.45 Bleu Raeders D12
6. 54.70 St. Paul Scouts
7. 53.00 St. John's All-girl

Exhibition
Racine Junior Scouts
Boys of '76
AmbassaDears
Kiltie Kadets

> *Goodwill celebration events Monday included a rain-interrupted Goodwill Spectacular Drum Corps Show sponsored by the Racine Boys of '76 Drum and Bugle Corps. A critique following the show reversed a decision on a one-point timing penalty and awarded first place to the Vanguards of Chicago with a 78.25. In second, after the critique, were the Racine Kilties who lost one-tenth of a point in penalties and scored 78.1. Other results: The Belleville, Ill. Black Knights, 72.25, the Racine Explorers, 69.70; the Bleu Raiders of New Orleans, 69.45; the St. Paul Scouts, 54.70; and the St. John's All-Girl Corps of Bedford, Canada, 53.00. The show had the Racine Scouts and the Kiltie Kadets in exhibition before-hand, and the Racine Elks Youth Band performing at the conclusion.*
> —Racine Journal Times, *July 5, 1972*

July 29—Music on the March

The show had only one DCI finalist and corps from three states. The Kewanee Black Knights junior drum and bugle corps was formed in 1965 when the longtime Kewanee Black Knights senior corps folded. In 1973, the corps moved to Geneseo and became the Geneseo Knights. It later moved to western Illinois and became the Quad City Knights. The corps appeared in Horlick Field under all its names.

JULY 29, 1972—MUSIC ON THE MARCH

1. 79.6 Kilties D8
2. 79.4 Kewanee Black Knights
3. 69.9 St. Paul Scouts
4. 68.9 Oshkosh Warriors
5. 59.5 Mariners
6. 55.7 Marquis
7. 40.4 32nd Hussars

Exhibition

Racine Scouts
Racine Junior Scouts

AUGUST 19—SENIOR SPECTACULAR

Corps Ready Sr. Spectacular
Senior East Coast drum corps will make their first appearances in the Midwest in some 15 years in an 11-corps show at 6:30 p.m. Saturday at Horlick Athletic Field. Racine's Boys of '76, a senior class drum and bugle corps, is sponsoring the "Senior Spectacular."

Featured corps will be the Hawthorne, N.J. Caballeros, 11 times national American Legion senior corps champions. The show will also include junior open class corps, with the Racine Kilties making their first hometown appearance since winning the World open in Boston two weeks ago. Other senior Eastern corps performing will be the Crusaders of Rochester, N.Y., and the Rockets of Pittsburgh, Pa. Brass Incorporated of St. Paul, Minn., will also participate.

"It's the first time any of the Eastern seniors have been in the Midwest for 15 years," said Gerald Hardy, president of the "Boys of '76." From the way tickets are selling, Hardy said, it looks like the audience will be "more of a Midwestern drum corps fan crowd. We're selling tickets to people from Michigan, Illinois, Minnesota, and Iowa quite regularly." The corps is hoping for an audience of 10,000 but at any rate "it looks like it will be pretty packed." The senior corps, Hardy said, "are the pinnacle of drum corps entertainment. They do entertain." The Hawthorne group

BOYS OF '76
SENIOR SPECTACULAR
SAT., AUGUST 19
6:30 p.m.
HORLICK FIELD

SENIORS	JUNIORS
HAWTHORNE CABALLEROS	BLUE STARS
CONNECTICUT HURRICANES	KILTIES
ROCHESTER CRUSADERS	RACINE EXPLORERS
PITTSBURGH ROCKETS	ST. PATRICK IMPERIALS
BRASS INC. ST. PAUL	MARINERS

TICKETS: Reserve $5.00
General Admission $4.00

TICKETS AVAILABLE AT: Charles Realty, 1235 Douglas Ave.; Guy Lloyd, Inc., 1644 Washington Ave.; King Ehrlich, 4101 Washington; Johnson's Music, 1409 Washington Ave.; King Ehrlich, 3121 North Main St.

marches with more than 70 horns, plus a 20-man drum line and a 20-man color guard, Hardy said.

The junior open class corps, mostly from the Midwest, that will be performing, include the Racine Explorers, the Blue Stars of La Crosse, and St. Patrick's Imperials of Milwaukee, the St. Andrew's Bridgemen of Bayonne, N.J., the Mariners of Milwaukee and the Kilties. There will also be a "surprise corps," Hardy said.

—Racine Journal Times, *August 18, 1972*

To many who were at this show, including several Drum Corps Hall of Fame members, the August 19, 1972 Senior Spectacular was the best drum and bugle corps show of all time. It is indisputably the best show ever in Horlick Field. The day after the first DCI finals in nearby Whitewater, 1972 DCA champion Hawthorne Caballeros and DCA finalists Rochester Crusaders and Pittsburgh Rockets joined eight junior corps—four of them DCI finalists—in an all-exhibition show in Horlick Field. Other DCI finalist drum corps sat in the audience as paying customers.

The Horlick Field audience had heard of and had records of the great eastern senior corps and was excited to see them for the first time. For the senior corps, it was an unjudged rehearsal before the American Legion Championships in Chicago the next night. To the junior corps that had finished second and third at the first DCI championship finals the night before, it was a chance to show that they should have won. Since it was an exhibition, all the corps let loose and went for audience reaction, and the audience reacted.

Corps members speak of the unbelievable screaming of the audience. Members of the audience speak of the greatest drum and bugle corps performances of all time.

Sometimes it all comes together, and this show was it for Horlick Field: the compact, intimate environment; the knowledgeable and appreciative audience; and big, loud, talented drum and bugle corps. It was a special night in drum and bugle corps history and in Horlick Field. The likes of it may never be seen again.

August 19, 1972—Senior Spectacular

Senior Exhibition

Hawthorne Caballeros DCA1
Rochester Crusaders DCA4
Pittsburgh Rockets.. DCA10
Minnesota Brass, Inc.

Junior Exhibition

Blue Stars D2
Santa Clara Vanguard D3
Kilties D8
St. Andrew's Bridgemen.. D11
Racine Scouts
St. Patrick's Imperials
Mariners
Boys of '76

St. Andrew's Bridgemen, 1972. *Photo by Jane Boulen, from the collection of* Drum Corps World.

A Rochester Crusader Memory

When we pulled in to the parking lot, all we could see was busses from all the great junior corps. DCI was the night before in Whitewater and we found out that several of them were there just to watch the show. We saw the Troopers busses and thought that they were going to perform, but they were just there to watch. Garfield bought tickets just to watch, too.

Sixty seconds into our show as we got off the line, we realized that the audience was something special. They were amazing, just screaming and

Hawthorne Caballeros, 1972. *Photo by Jane Boulen, from the collection of* Drum Corps World.

yelling through the whole show. Their applause and reaction was incredible. It brought out a performance that was second to none. We were busting our buttons, flying four feet off the ground. None of us have ever forgotten it.

*One of the fondest memories of the show, after concert, we came out playing Battle Hymn and at the end, it goes real soft, and when it went quiet, some kid in the audience yelled out as loud as he could, "Ho-o-oly ****!"*

At the alumni events, everyone remembers the show. I talk about it often and say that it's one of the finest, if not the *finest, performance Rochester ever did. And the guys from Hawthorne say the same thing.*

The winners that night were the performers on the field and the people in the stands. It was the intimacy of the place that was special, being able to relate to the audience, it was just amazing.

—Tom Peashey, Rochester Crusaders, 1972; Drum Corps Hall of Fame, 2006

Chapter 16

A Two–Drum Corps Exhibition

1973

1973 Statistics

Number of shows..2
Drum corps performances..........................11
States represented.......................................6
Championship finalist performances.............6

The year 1973 saw the fewest drum and bugle corps performances since 1961, which had only one show. Even with the low number of drum corps performances, the shows had good variety, with corps from six states and two from Canada. After the amazing eastern senior corps exhibition of 1972, the New York Skyliners booked an exhibition of its own, as noted in the newspaper ad, but in the end did not make the trip. The July 3 Goodwill Spectacular was the Troopers' tenth appearance and fifth win in Horlick Field since the corps first appeared in 1963.

A third show, the June 16 Music on the March, was rained out and held as a standstill. The seven corps in the event were the Blue Stars, Kilties, Belleville Black Knights, Boys of '76, Marion Cadets, Racine Scouts and Racine Junior Scouts.

July 3—Goodwill Spectacular

The 1973 Goodwill Spectacular had nine drum corps, four DCI finalists, corps from four states and two corps from Canada. The corps that appeared were iconic: Troopers, Kilties, Belleville Black Knights, Argonne Rebels and Toronto Optimists.

The Toronto Optimists appeared for the first time since the 1964 East-West Spectacular. The New Day was a continuation of the AmbassaDears and remained under the new name until it folded in about 1997.

Belleville Black Knights, 1973. The corps wore a series of distinctive uniforms that had one white and one black sleeve. *Courtesy of Moe Knox.*

JULY 3, 1973—GOODWILL SPECTACULAR

1. 80.4 Troopers D2
2. 79.1 Kilties D5
3. 75.0 Belleville Black Knights D10
4. 64.8 Argonne Rebels D11
5. 61.5 Toronto Optimists

Exhibition

Racine Junior Scouts
Kiltie Kadets
New Day
Dutch Boy Cadets

AUGUST 15—DCI PREVIEW

The following description of this show was written by George D. Fennell and intended for his book *We Winna Be Dauntit!* but did not make it into the printed copy. Courtesy of George D. Fennell.

> *At 7:00 p.m. on Wednesday, August 15, 1973, a show billed as a "DCI Preview" was held at Racine's Horlick Field. This show was short and sweet. Only two drum and bugle corps, the Anaheim Kingsmen from Orange County, California, and the Kilties performed exhibitions. There was no*

HORLICK FIELD 7:00
wed.
august
15......
ADULTS $1.00
CHILDREN under 12 $.50
d.c.i.
preview
Anaheim Kingsmen
1972 DRUM CORPS INTERNATIONAL CHAMPS
& Racine Kilties
TOP CONTENDERS FOR 1973

competition, nor were there any other performances of any kind. Tickets were $1.00 for adults and $0.50 for children.

This show was made possible through the cooperation of the Racine Park and Recreation Dept. and the Tuesday Optimist Club of Racine. Proceeds went to the Tuesday Optimists Boys Work Fund.

August 15, 1973—DCI Preview

Exhibition

Kilties D5
Anaheim Kingsmen D6

Chapter 17

Twenty-three Shows in Five Years

1974–1978

The years 1974 to 1978 were the busiest in Horlick Field's long history of hosting drum and bugle corps. It hosted twenty-three shows, an average of almost five a year. It seemed as if one could not book enough shows in Horlick Field to fill both the insatiable appetite of the Horlick Field audience to see drum corps and the desire of drum and bugle corps to perform there.

It was also a period of unparalleled quality of the drum and bugle corps in the shows. In the five years, Horlick Field hosted one show with the top four DCI corps, another with the top three and another with the top two. Overall, it hosted an average of almost thirty-five drum and bugle corps performances per year.

It was the last blast of glory; 1979 began the long decline to irrelevance.

1974–1978 Statistics

Number of shows..23
Drum corps performances..........................173*
DCI champion performances.........................4
Championship finalist performances...........44
*The corps that appeared at the 1977 Music on the March were unknown at the time of printing.

Chapter 18

Four Contests and the National Champion

1974

1974 Statistics

Number of shows..4
Drum corps performances............................37
States represented...6
National champion performances...................1
Championship finalist performances.............7

In 1974, Horlick Field hosted one very good and three average shows. There was a large Class C show and open class shows with one, two and four DCI finalists. Two California corps and one from Delaware appeared. Eight drum corps appeared in Horlick Field for the first time, and the Spectacle City Mariners and Anaheim Kingsmen appeared for the last time.

July 3—Goodwill Spectacular

The Spectacular in 1974 had only one championship finalist, and most of the corps scored under fifty points. The Skokie Imperials was a continuation of the Norwood Park Imperials, which had first appeared at the Racine Scouts Twenty-fifth Anniversary show in 1952. This was its twelfth appearance in Horlick Field.

This was the first appearance in Horlick Field by the Pioneer, formed by the merger of the Mercury Thunderbolts and the St. Patrick's Imperials in

Pioneer, 1974. *From the collection of* Drum Corps World.

late 1972. In 1973, the merged corps was known as the Thing. It took on the name Pioneer in 1974.

JULY 3, 1974—GOODWILL SPECTACULAR

1. 72.85 Kilties D6
2. 58.40 Pioneer
3. 44.90 Mariners
4. 31.65 Queen City Cadets
5. Skokie Imperials

Exhibition

New Day
Racine Junior Scouts
Kiltie Kadets

July 13—Music on the March

This was an average Horlick Field show with eight corps, two of them DCI finalists. The Audubon Bon Bons, perhaps the best all-girl drum corps of all time, was advertised but did not appear.

This was the seventh appearance in Horlick Field by the Americanos. The corps would appear two more straight years. The corps had previously appeared in Horlick Field three years in a row between 1957 and 1959.

This was Mariners' ninth appearance in seven years and the second in 1974. The Mariners disbanded at the end of 1974.

July 13, 1974—Music on the March

Class C*

Madison Junior Scouts
New Dawn
Kiltie Kadets
*Scores and places unknown

Class A

1. 75.80 Kilties D6
2. 72.40 Phantom Regiment D11
3. 60.50 Americanos
4. 59.65 Pioneer
5. 59.60 Blue Rock
6. 39.00 Mariners

Exhibition

Boys of '76
Racine Scouts

July 21—Horns-a-Plenty

Five drum corps made their first appearances in Horlick Field at this show, reflecting the rapid growth in the number of drum and bugle corps during the period. New corps seemed to spring up everywhere. This Class C show had eleven drum corps, all of them from mid-central to southern Wisconsin, and most of them were still new. CapitolAires was formed in 1971, Windjammers and Wausau Story in 1973 and the West Bend Patriots and CapitolAire Petites in the same period. Most of the new corps formed in this sudden growth would last only a few years.

July 21, 1974—Horns-a-Plenty

1. 60.10 CapitolAires
2. 57.75 Windjammers
3. 39.35 CapitolAire Petites
4. 39.25 Belles of St. Mary's
5. 39.10 Wausau Story
6. 38.50 Kiltie Kadets
7. 35.40 Madison Junior Scouts
8. 31.25 West Bend Patriots
9. 29.40 Racine Junior Scouts

Exhibition

New Dawn

New Day

JULY 28—CAPITAL OF CORPS CHAMPIONSHIP

This was a very good show, with the top three DCI drum corps in 1974 and four of the top six, and it had two California corps, which was still somewhat notable in the Midwest. There were few touring California corps, and they could make only a select few Midwest appearances. It was Anaheim Kingsmen's fifth appearance in six years and its last appearance in Horlick Field.

The Blue Notes was from Ishpeming, in the Upper Peninsula of Michigan, where it competed against the Munising Silver Echoes, Ontonagon Mountaineers, L'Anse Golden Eagles and Menominee Northernaires. The corps rarely competed as far away as southern Wisconsin. This was the Blue Notes' second of only two appearances in Horlick Field.

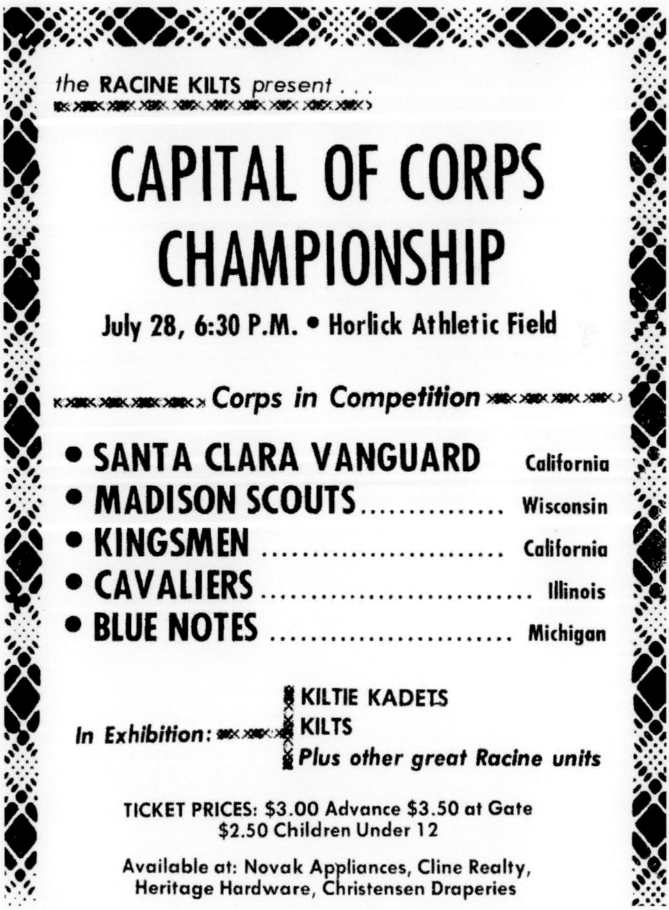

Kilties in Horlick Field, 1974. *Photo by Michael T. Pendell, from the collection of George D. Fennell.*

JULY 28, 1974—CAPITAL OF CORPS CHAMPIONSHIP

1. 83.65 Santa Clara Vanguard D1
2. 83.15 Madison Scouts D2
3. 80.50 Anaheim Kingsmen D3
4. 72.95 Cavaliers D8
5. 43.85 Ishpeming Blue Notes

Exhibition

Kiltie Kadets

Kilties D6

Chapter 19

The Top Three in One Show for the Second Year in a Row

1975

1975 Statistics

Number of shows...4
Drum corps performances............................31
States represented 7
DCI champion performances.........................1
Championship finalist performances 11

Horlick Field hosted two great shows, an average show and a Class C show in 1975. Seven drum corps appeared in Horlick Field for the first time.

July 3—Goodwill Spectacular

The Kilties in 1975 was a prime example of the top corps of the day: well over one hundred members, very high average age, extremely experienced and talented members and tremendously loud. Drum and bugle corps of the day had ear-splitting volume, and people roared back nearly as loudly. The Kilties was a contender for the DCI title all summer but fell to seventh place at finals.

Finleyville Royal Crusaders was formed in 1969 and quickly rose to prominence. It finished sixteenth and seventeenth in the 1973 and 1974 DCI championships and jumped to ninth in 1975. Like many of the new corps formed in the late '60s and '70s, it folded after a few years of existence. Minnesota Brass was formed in 1969 and first performed in Horlick Field at the senior exhibition show in 1972. It appeared in Horlick Field eleven times overall. This was the Troopers' eleventh appearance. It would not return for six years.

July 3, 1975—Goodwill Spectacular

Juniors

1. 69.40 Kilties D7
2. 69.30 Finleyville Royal Crusaders D9
3. 67.95 Phantom Regiment D10
4. 62.75 Toronto Optimists
5. 59.20 Troopers D12
6. 34.40 Mounties

Seniors

1. 48.10 Minnesota Brass, Inc.
2. 44.45 Boys of '76

Exhibition

Kiltie Kadets
New Dawn

July 11—Music on the March

The Fond du Lac, Wisconsin Marquis, formed in 1969, rose to sixteenth place at DCI in 1976 and spent its last years as a Class C corps before folding in 1985. At the time of this show, it was big, had a good show and was on the rise. The Fox Valley Raiders was formed in 1971 and rose as high as twenty-eighth at DCI prelims in 1977 but folded at the end of 1977.

July 11, 1975—Music on the March

1. 75.60 Kilties D7
2. 65.75 Marquis
3. 59.40 Americanos
4. 49.80 Fox Valley Raiders
5. 35.25 Scarlet Knights

Exhibition

Racine Scouts
Racine Junior Scouts

August 3—Capital of Corps Championships

This was a great show in any year. It had the top three DCI corps of the year and six of the top eight DCI finalists. Like the Goodwill Spectacular of 1962, all the corps in competition and one in exhibition made championship finals. The night before, at DCI Midwest in Whitewater, the top three corps in the show were spread by 2.7 points, but at this show, the corps were only 0.55 points apart, an indication of how hotly contested and exciting the show was.

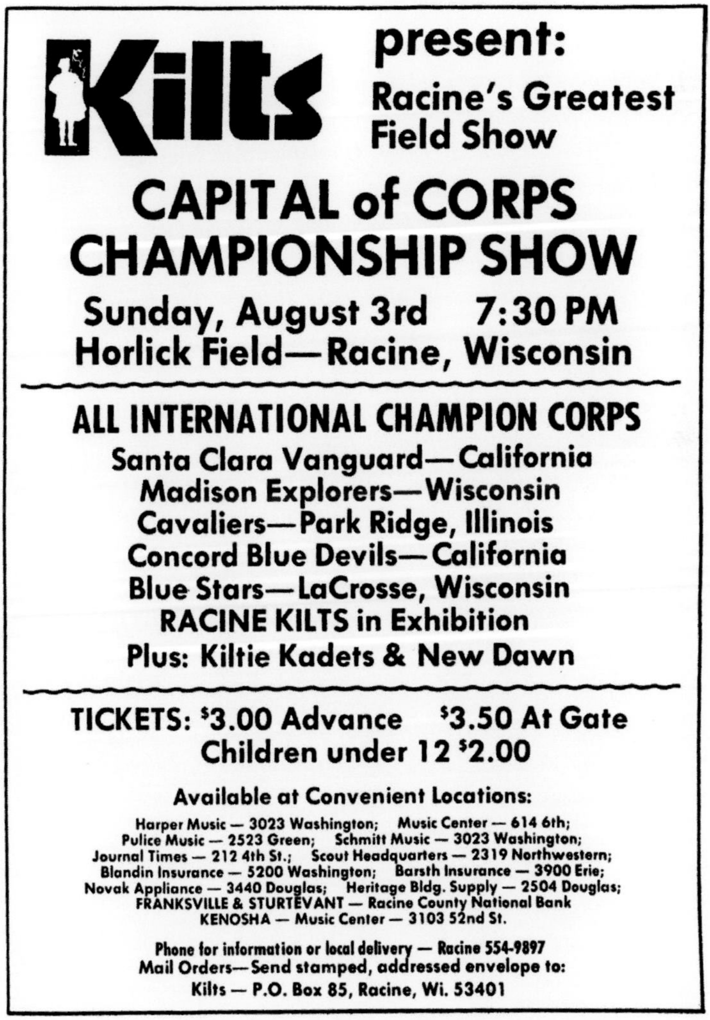

August 3, 1975—Capital of Corps Championship

1. 85.50 Madison Scouts....D1
2. 85.10 Santa Clara Vanguard....D2
3. 84.95 Blue Devils....D3
4. 84.20 Blue Stars....D5
5. 78.35 Cavaliers....D8

Exhibition

Kilties....D7
Kiltie Kadets
New Dawn

Youth, Racine benefit from superb Kiltie show

Any event attractive enough to lure 5,000 witnesses on a beautiful summer night is worthy of comment.

The Kilts' "Capital of Corps Championship Show" Sunday night at Horlick Field was such an occurrence—3½ hours of delightful and thoroughly entertaining music and showmanship. In an era of dull and sex-ridden entertainment on the movie screens, endless and boring reruns on television and very little family activity in most communities, Sunday night's drum and bugle corps competition was an entertainment bonanza.

The crowd loved it. Men, women and children rose with crescendos of applause and salutes as defending national champion the Santa Clara, Calif., Vanguard, the Madison Scouts, the Park Ridge, Ill., Cavaliers, the Concord, Calif., Blue Devils and La Crosse Blue Stars sparkled with intricate formations and maneuvers.

Madison's explosive corps was judged the victor and the hometown New Dawn, Kiltie Kadets and Racine Kilties provided bonuses with exhibition performances.

Good, solid entertainment. It was youth at its best. These young men and women are the real youth of today—well behaved, well-guided and leaders of tomorrow—not the exceptions on the police blotters or school delinquents.

Thank you. Not only for the superb entertainment, but for contributing to a better community.

—Racine Journal Times, *August 5, 1975*

August 9—Belle City Drum Corps "75"

The six Class C corps in this show are indicative of how strong the drum and bugle corps activity was at the time. Most top-level drum and bugle corps had large feeder units that were regionally competitive. The Midwest held many Class C–only shows each summer that each fielded a lot of entertaining units.

August 9, 1975—Belle City Drum Corps "75"*
Cavalier Cadets
Imperial Cadets
Men of Brass junior
Nisei Ambassadors
CapitolAire Petites
Princemen
*Scores and places are unknown.

Chapter 20

The Top Four in One Show

1976

1976 Statistics

Number of shows	5
Drum corps performances	41
States represented	6
DCI champion performances	1
Championship finalist performances	8

In the bicentennial year, Horlick Field hosted five shows in one year for the first time. Horlick Field hosted one great show with DCI's top four corps of 1976, the first senior contest in ten years and three average contests.

July 3—Twenty-fifth Annual Spectacular

The Twenty-fifth Annual Spectacular show had two senior corps and three junior corps in competition. Only one DCI finalist appeared, the twelfth-place Guardsmen. A total of seven corps from three states performed. The Guardsmen, formed in 1961, made its first appearance in DCI finals in 1976 after finishing thirty-first at DCI in 1975. This was the Americanos' seventh appearance in Horlick Field. The corps had first appeared at the 1946 American Legion State Championship, thirty years earlier.

July 3, 1976—Twenty-fifth Annual Spectacular

Senior

1. 41.75 Minnesota Brass, Inc.
2. 41.55 Spirit of '76

Junior

1. 70.30 Guardsmen..D12
2. 62.45 Americanos
3. 55.05 Pioneer

Exhibition

Kiltie Kadets
New Day

July 11—Music on the March

The Marquis beat the Blue Stars by 1.4 points at this show, but one month later, at DCI prelims, Blue Stars took ninth, beating the Marquis, in sixteenth, by over 5.0 points. The Chicago Vanguard was the last name assumed by the historic Logan Square/Mel Tierney/Skokie/Des Plaines Vanguard organization that had first appeared in Horlick Field in 1952. The corps finished as high as third at VFW finals in 1967 and was in the first DCI top twelve in 1972. But the corps fell to twentieth in 1973 and forty-first in 1975. This was the corps' tenth and last appearance in Horlick Field. It folded after 1978. A senior corps of the same name appeared in 1990. The advertised Toronto Optimists did not appear.

July 11, 1976—Music on the March

1. 71.40 Marquis
2. 70.00 Blue Stars D9
3. 56.45 Kilties
4. 55.55 Chicago Vanguard
5. 50.55 Pioneer
6. 48.90 Colt 45s

Exhibition

Racine Scouts
Kiltie Kadets

JULY 18—BELLE CITY DRUM CORPS "76"

The show had eleven corps from three states, but the winning corps, Marion Cadets, took only twenty-seventh at DCI prelims. The Norwood Park Imperials had become the Skokie Imperials in the early '70s. The corps appeared in Horlick Field thirteen times and won two shows, in 1965 and 1966. This was its last appearance in Horlick Field. It had first appeared in 1952.

July 18, 1976—Belle City Drum Corps "76"
1. 68.10 Marion Cadets
2. 66.60 Fox Valley Raiders
3. 55.00 Vaqueros
4. 43.60 Skokie Imperials

Class C
1. 44.55 Kiltie Kadets
2. 30.80 Guardsmen Cadets
3. 24.30 CapitolAire Petites
4. 22.15 New Dawn
5. 19.95 Imperial Cadets

Exhibition
New Day

AUGUST 8—TWO SHOWS IN ONE DAY

> *Sound of music*
> *The blare of brass and the sound of drums resounded through Horlick Field Sunday afternoon as six of the area's top Class C Drum and Bugle Corps performed in "Brigadoon" competition. The event was sponsored by the Kiltie Kadets. Also performing in the afternoon were the Kilts, who hosted their own "Capitol of Corps Championship" in the evening. That performance featured several former Drum Corps International (DCI) champions, including the Santa Clara, Calif., Vanguards; the Madison Scouts; the Concord, Calif., Blue Devils; and the Etobicoke Crusaders, Etobicoke, Ont., Can.*
> —Racine Journal Times, *August 9, 1976*

In previous years, the Kilties and Kiltie Kadets had held their shows on different days. In 1976, 1977, 1978 and 1980, the two drum corps hosted their shows on the same day. The Kadets' show was in the early afternoon, while the Kilties' show was at night. In 1978, one ticket allowed entry to both shows; in the other three years, each show had separate tickets.

August 8—Brigadoon

Six Class C drum and bugle corps competed in the Kiltie Kadet afternoon show, but only the Kiltie Kadets and the Phantom Regiment Cadets have been identified.

August 8, 1976—Brigadoon*
Kiltie Kadets
Phantom Regiment Cadets
Exhibition
Kilties
*Places and the other four corps in the show are unknown.

August 8—Capital of Corps

The 1976 Capital of Corps contest was a spectacular show, another mini-nationals. It had the top four DCI corps, six of the top eight and eleven corps total. This was the second time that Horlick Field hosted a show with the top four corps of the year. Madison finished fourth at this show, over seven points behind the Blue Devils. Thirteen days later, it took second at DCI, less than a point behind. This was the third appearance in Horlick Field in 1976 by the Pioneer.

August 8, 1976—Capital of Corps Championship
1. 90.60 Blue Devils D1
2. 84.75 Phantom Regiment D4
3. 83.75 Santa Clara Vanguard D3
4. 83.35 Madison Scouts D2
5. 81.15 Cavaliers.. D7

6. 81.05 Etobicoke Crusaders D8
7. 65.05 Pioneer

Exhibition

Kiltie Kadets
Kilties

Chapter 21

The Most Shows in One Year

1977

1977 Statistics

Number of shows..6
Drum corps performances..35+ (the corps in the August 20 Music on the March were unknown at the time of printing)
States represented..7
Championship finalist performances..........................6

There were six shows in Horlick Field in 1977, the most ever. There were a senior championship show, a senior-junior show, three junior shows and a Class C show. One corps that appeared in Horlick Field this year placed in finals but was disqualified, otherwise Horlick Field would have hosted seven finalist performances in 1977 and perhaps the DCI champion.

July 3—Spectacular

Drum and bugle corps were becoming more expensive to host. As a result, fewer drum corps appeared in each show, and this show is proof.

Horlick Field shows in the 1960s and early 1970s almost always had ten or more corps performing; this show had six. The Kilties won the show and took eleventh at DCI. The Marquis took twenty-sixth at DCI and folded at the end of the year. This was Minnesota Brass, Inc.'s fourth time in Horlick Field and its third straight win; its first appearance was an exhibition.

JULY 3, 1977—SPECTACULAR
1. 72.20 Kilties 11
2. 62.60 Marquis
3. 55.10 Marion Cadets
4. 50.70 Cleveland Caballeros
Seniors
1. 59.05 Minnesota Brass, Inc.
2. 51.70 Spirit of '76

JULY 17—BELLE CITY DRUM CORPS "77"

This show had eight corps from four states. Geneseo Knights took thirty-eighth at DCI prelims in 1977. It was Marion Cadets' second win in Horlick Field and fourth and last appearance. It had first appeared in 1962.

JULY 17, 1977—BELLE CITY DRUM CORPS "77"
1. 59.70 Marion Cadets
2. 57.00 Geneseo Knights
3. 47.40 Valiant Knights
4. 40.45 Kiltie Kadets
5. 35.25 Mercury Thunderbolts
6. 23.75 Colonels
Exhibition
New Dawn
New Day

AUGUST 7—BRIGADOON

During this period, the Kiltie Kadets participated in and hosted Cadet Corps International (CCI) shows. Because many Class A corps of the era had large feeder units, CCI was very active at this time and hosted several shows each summer.

AUGUST 7, 1977—BRIGADOON
1. 53.25 Madison Junior Scouts
2. 47.60 Cavalier Cadets
3. 46.80 Kiltie Kadets
4. 34.80 Wausau Pages
5. 29.05 Guardsmen Cadets
6. 28.85 Phantom Regiment Cadets
7. 14.30 Imperial Cadets

Exhibition
Kilties D11

AUGUST 7—CAPITAL OF CORPS CHAMPIONSHIP

When St. Andrew's Bridgemen first appeared in Horlick Field in 1972, it wore cadet uniforms and had military demeanor and precision, representative of most drum corps of the day. In 1977, the Bridgemen (without the saint) returned to Horlick Field with a completely different identity. By then, many corps had taken advantage of the freedom allowed by DCI rules and had developed wildly original, entertaining shows with costumes, props and dancing. The 1977 Bridgemen was at the forefront and was extremely popular.

The Bridgemen won this show by over a point and was a leading contender to win the DCI championship but was disqualified from DCI championships for age issues. Phantom Regiment, which lost to Bridgemen in this show, took second at DCI finals. While this show had five DCI finalist performances, if the Bridgemen had not been disqualified, the show would have had six finalists and may have had the DCI champion. In any case, this show had three of the top four corps of the year, two other finalists and the fifteenth-place Guardsmen.

August 7, 1977—Capital of Corps Championship

1. 87.50 Bridgemen
2. 86.45 Phantom Regiment D2
3. 84.30 Madison Scouts D5
4. 80.30 Guardsmen
5. 79.45 Cavaliers D7

Exhibition

Kilties D11
Kiltie Kadets

August 20—Music on the March

August 20, 1977—Music on the March

Corps unknown at time of printing

Exhibition

Racine Scouts

August 27—Mid-States Senior Association Championship Show

MID-STATES SENIOR ASSOCIATION
FIRST ANNUAL SENIOR DRUM & BUGLE CORPS

CHAMPIONSHIP

AUGUST 27, 1977
7:00 P.M.

HORLICK FIELD
1648 N. Memorial Dr.

COMPETING CORPS

BRASS, INC.
Minneapolis, Mn.

GOVERNAIRES
St. Peter, Mn.

CHICAGO CONNECTION
Wheeling, Il.

SPIRIT OF '76
Racine, Wi.

EXHIBITION BY THE KILTIE KADETS OF RACINE

TICKETS • $2.50 AT GATE • $2.00 ADVANCE • $1.50 CHILDREN

SCHONERTS INC.
1659 N. Main

SCHMITT MUSIC
1409 Washington

CHARLES REALTY
1235 Douglas

GUY LLOYD
1650 Washington

KING ERHLICH
4101 Washington
3921 N. Main

This was a decent Midwest senior show but had only five drum corps. Chicago Connection took eleventh and Minnesota Brass, Inc. took twelfth at DCA prelims, only 0.35 behind.

August 27, 1977—Mid-States Senior Association Championship Show*

Minnesota Brass, Inc.
Govenaires
Chicago Connection
Spirit of '76
Exhibition
Kiltie Kadets
*Scores are unknown.

Chapter 22

The End of an Era

1978

1978 Statistics

Number of shows	4
Drum corps performances	29
States represented	7
DCI champion performances	1
Championship finalist performances	12

The year 1978 was the last of the great years of Horlick Field and was exemplary of the whole. It hosted four shows, twenty-nine drum and bugle corps performances, the national champion and a total of twelve finalists. The statistics are remarkably similar to the first of the great years, 1962, which hosted three shows, twenty-eight performances, the national champion and fourteen finalists. Together, they are bookends that represent an era.

June 24—VFW State Championships

This show had six corps, all from Wisconsin, and two DCI finalists. Wausau Story was another corps that was formed, rose quickly to top-twenty-five status and then folded during the 1970s. It won DCI Class A championship in 1976, its first year at DCI. It finished twenty-fifth in open class 1978. The Sundowners was a co-ed continuation of the Eau Claire Boy Scouts/Eau Claire Boys drum corps that was formed as a band in 1952 and became a drum and bugle corps in about 1957. This was the fourteenth appearance of the Pioneer drum and bugle corps organization, eight times as St. Patrick's Imperials and six times as the Pioneer.

June 24, 1978—VFW State Championship

1. 70.05 Blue Stars D8
2. 64.85 Kilties D12
3. 57.05 Wausau Story
4. 41.40 CapitolAires
5. 39.95 Pioneer
6. 36.65 Sundowners

July 3—Goodwill Spectacular

This nine-corps show had three DCI finalists, one corps from California and one from Colorado. The two senior corps took twelfth and thirteenth at DCA championships but were eleven and fourteen points, respectively, from a finals slot. This was the last year that the Kilties made DCI finals. It fell to thirty-second place in 1979 and did not compete in 1980. The drum corps in the show came from five different states.

July 3, 1978—Goodwill Spectacular

1. 78.40 Madison Scouts D4
2. 72.15 Blue Stars D8
3. 65.75 Kilties D12
4. 49.30 Blue Knights

Senior

1. 47.85 Minnesota Brass, Inc.
2. 44.75 Chicago Connection

Exhibition
Conquistadors
Scarlet Knights
Kiltie Kadets

July 16—Cadet Corps International Contest

As in the 1977 Kiltie Kadet show, all the competing drum corps were Cadet-class units that were feeder units to DCI-class corps.

JULY 16, 1978—CADET CORPS INTERNATIONAL CONTEST

1. 47.25 Madison Junior Scouts
2. 43.05 Cavalier Cadets
3. 37.50 Kiltie Kadets
4. 33.85 Phantom Regiment Cadets
5. 27.50 Wausau Pages
6. 19.65 Colt Cadets

Exhibition

Kilties D12

JULY 16—CAPITAL OF CORPS CHAMPIONSHIP

This was the last of the great shows in Horlick Field. The show had six DCI championship finalist drum corps, including the top two corps. Every drum corps in the open-class show made DCI finals. Spirit of Atlanta was the surprise hit of the summer, with a big, wall-of-sound repertoire written by the legendary Jim Ott. The corps had first appeared at DCI championship in 1977 in twenty-second place and rose to sixth in 1978. Spirit lost to the Crossmen by one point at this show but, a month later at DCI finals, beat the Crossmen by over four points.

Santa Clara Vanguard, which won this show, had taken fourth place the night before at DCI Midwest in Whitewater, 1.6 points behind the first-place Phantom Regiment. Phantom Regiment won nine of its remaining twelve shows, including a tie for first at DCI prelims. The Vanguard won only three more shows all summer, but one of them was the DCI championship finals.

JULY 16, 1978—CAPITAL OF CORPS CHAMPIONSHIP

Open Class

1. 86.20 Santa Clara Vanguard D1
2. 86.10 Phantom Regiment D2
3. 81.60 Crossmen D9
4. 80.55 Spirit of Atlanta D6
5. 71.05 Guardsmen D11

Exhibition

Kilties D12
Kiltie Kadets

Santa Clara Vanguard, Horlick Field, July 16, 1978. *Photo by Emil Anello, from the collection of Jim Anello.*

The picture above gives you a sense of the closeness of the performers and the audience. The view is from halfway up the stands, but the vantage is still very close to the performers.

Chapter 23

THE LONG DECLINE

1979 AND BEYOND

The end of the period of greatness of Horlick Field is easy to identify. Between 1974 and 1978, Horlick Field hosted 23 drum and bugle corps shows with more than 173 drum corps performances, an average of 34 per year. Between 1979 and 1983, Horlick Field hosted 10 shows with 61 drum and bugle corps performances, an average of 12 per year.

A single statistic reveals the change in Horlick Field's status in the drum and bugle corps activity. Horlick Field hosted a total of 158 championship finalist performances in the seventeen years from 1962 through 1978. In the thirty-five years from 1979 through 2013, Horlick Field hosted only 24 performances by a DCI championship contest finalist. In comparison, in 1969 alone, Horlick Field hosted 16 finalist performances.

The times had changed. DCI had functioned for seven years and had begun to arrange group tours for its units. DCI demanded more money for a DCI package of drum and bugle corps to appear, and that required higher ticket prices and large arenas. Horlick Field, with only 7,500 seats, was at a disadvantage.

The long decline began. There were years without any show. In the 1980s, a few drum and bugle corps shows were held in Pershing Park, along the lakefront in downtown Racine. In the early 2000s, several shows were held at Case High School, which is closer to the freeway and has a huge, easy-to-get-to parking lot. Not surprisingly, the old school Horlick Field fans did not follow. The other fields lacked the intimacy, character and overall experience of Horlick Field. Pershing Park is often cold and damp in the evening. Case High School has a wide track, and the grandstands are well away from the field.

And you can't buy beer at Pershing Park or Case High School.

June 23, 1979—Music on the March

It was a very cold day, power was out in Horlick Field due to an automobile accident nearby and only about one hundred people were in the audience for this Class C show. The host Racine Scouts chose to not perform an exhibition.

June 23, 1979—Music on the March
1. 41.15 Memorial Lancers
2. 38.05 West Bend Patriots
3. 35.40 Mercury Thunderbolts
4. 30.10 Kiltie Kadets
5. 27.20 Silver Spectrum

Exhibition
Spirit of '76

July 3, 1979—Spectacular

After Minnesota Brass, Inc. performed, the show was rained out. This was one of only three shows ever rained out in Horlick Field.

July 3, 1979—Spectacular
1. 47.15 Minnesota Brass, Inc.

July 13, 1979—Capital of Corps Championship

This was the third and last appearance in Horlick Field by the Bridgemen. It was a good show, with two finalists and an old favorite, the Boston Crusaders, which took nineteenth place at DCI prelims in a time when being in the top twenty-five still meant that you were a loud and entertaining drum and bugle corps.

During the years around this show, Boston Crusaders was a nationwide crowd favorite because it almost defiantly held to its traditional East Coast style and music in the face of the radical changes that DCI was encouraging. In every performance, Boston Crusaders received a loud and long-standing ovation when it played its signature chart, "Conquest." People knew it was coming and were always thrilled when it came. Boston appeared in Horlick Field three times overall, in 1964, 1979 and 2008.

The Guardsmen made DCI finals in 1976, 1978, 1979 and 1980. Its highest finish was in 1979, when it took seventh. The corps may be most remembered for its very tall shakoes and its appearance in Kentucky Fried Chicken commercials with Colonel Sanders.

JULY 13, 1979—CAPITAL OF CORPS CHAMPIONSHIP

1. 78.45 Bridgemen..D6
2. 78.40 Guardsmen..D7
3. 69.20 Boston Crusaders
4. 56.05 Kilties

Exhibition

Kiltie Kadets

The Guardsmen, 1979. The Guardsmen appeared in Horlick Field twelve times. *From the collection of* Drum Corps World.

July 3, 1980—Fourth Fest Spectacular

This was the twenty-eighth Spectacular, but it was less than spectacular. Memphis Blues Brass Band is likely to have won this, its only show in Horlick Field, but no record of the scores or places was found. MB3, as it was known, had a brief life. It came out of nowhere to take twentieth at DCI preliminaries in 1980, finished eighteenth and nineteenth in the next two years and folded in 1983.

The Americanos took thirty-ninth and the First Canadian Regiment took forty-first at DCI in 1980. None of the three senior corps went to the DCA championships.

July 3, 1980—Fourth Fest Spectacular*

Senior

Minnesota Brass, Inc.
Chicago Connection
Spirit of '76

Junior

Memphis Blues Brass Band
Americanos
First Canadian Regiment

Exhibition

Kiltie Kadets
Racine Scouts

*Scores and places are unknown.

July 13, 1980—Brigadoon

In 1980, the Kilties and Kiltie Kadets again held their shows in Horlick Field on the same day. Brigadoon, Kiltie Kadet's Class C Cadet Corps International contest, was held in the early afternoon.

July 13, 1980—Brigadoon

1. 47.5 Kiltie Kadets
2. 33.7 Madison Junior Scouts
3. 32.7 Cavalier Cadets
4. 10.5 Los Charros

DRUM CORPS CONTESTS
SUNDAY, JULY 13
HORLICK FIELD
BRIGADOON SHOW-1:30 pm
In CADET Competition...
• Kiltie Kadets • Cavalier Cadets
• Madison Jr. Scouts • Los Charros
SCOTTISH SUPERSOUND-7 pm
In Open Competition...
• Phantom Regiment • Saginaires
• Cavaliers • Royal Grenadiers
• Pioneers • Emerald Knights
In Exhibition...
• Kiltie Kadets • Racine Explorers
TICKET INFORMATION...
AFTERNOON-$3 Adults, $1.50 Children
EVENING-Reserved, $6 (All ages)
Gen. Adm , $4 Adults
$3 Children
A DAY FOR THE WHOLE FAMILY
Sponsored By: Racine Kilts, Inc.

July 13, 1980—Scottish Supersound

This show had two DCI finalists and ten corps from four states. In the next five years, only one DCI finalist would perform in Horlick Field.

July 13, 1980—Scottish Supersound

Open Class

1. 83.5 Phantom Regiment D5
2. 77.2 Cavaliers.. D9
3. 55.5 Pioneer
4. 55.0 Saginaires
5. 35.9 Emerald Knights
6. 33.7 Royal Grenadiers

Exhibition

Racine Scouts
Kiltie Kadets

August 23, 1980—Cadet Corps International Championships

The 1980 Kiltie Kadets was a very good Class C corps that regularly defeated Class A corps during the summer. The corps was very popular, generated great crowd response and made the cover of *Drum Corps World*. This was the championship show of Cadet Corps International.

August 23, 1980—Cadet Corps International Championships

1. 57.15 Kiltie Kadets
2. 49.55 Cavalier Cadets
3. 47.35 Madison Junior Scouts
4. 39.15 Phantom Regiment Cadets
5. 15.50 Los Charros

July 4, 1981—Fourth Fest Spectacular

This show had only seven drum corps from three states and no DCI finalist. Even so, it was a pretty good show. Blue Stars, Guardsmen and Colts all finished in the top twenty-five at DCI, which meant that they were talented, entertaining drum corps; there were still a lot of high-quality units at the time. But the average score of the units in the show was below fifty points. The advertised Crossmen did not appear.

Spirit of '76 took fourteenth at DCA prelims, eleven points out of finals.

July 4, 1981—Fourth Fest Spectacular
Junior
1. 60.70 Blue Stars
2. 55.70 Guardsmen
3. 44.00 Colts
4. 40.40 Pioneer
5. 22.90 Vaqueros

Senior
1. 34.60 Minnesota Brass, Inc.
2. 29.05 Spirit of '76

Exhibition
Racine Scouts
Kiltie Kadets

August 7, 1981—One Night in August

The second show of 1981 had nine drum corps from five states. The Kilties appeared for the first time in Horlick Field since 1979; it was not active in 1980.

This was the crowd favorite Casper Troopers' first time in Horlick Field in six years and its twelfth time overall. The Troopers, which took twelfth at DCI in 1981, was the only championship finalist to perform in Horlick Field in 1981–82.

August 7, 1981—One Night in August
1. 76.25 Troopers..D12
2. 73.80 Guardsmen
3. 67.90 Seattle Imperials
4. 54.95 Pioneer
5. 43.45 Royal Grenadiers
6. 32.20 Vaqueros
7. 23.80 Statesmen

Exhibition

Kilties
Kiltie Kadets

July 3, 1982—Spectacular

Six corps appeared, and the high score was 47.9. The winning corps took thirtieth at DCI prelims.

July 3, 1982—Spectacular
1. 47.90 Saginaires
2. 44.40 Pioneer
3. 22.65 Kilties
4. 20.45 Wausau Story

Senior
1. 34.60 Ohio Brass Factory
2. 29.05 Spirit of '76

> *Saginaires, Brass Factory win in Racine*
> *by Steve Vickers*
> *To get Racine's Fourth of July weekend off to a big start, the senior Spirit of '76 hosted their annual drum corps competition in familiar Horlick Field. The combination junior/senior corps show saw the Michigan Saginaires top their portion of the contest over the Pioneer and the two-corps senior competition had Brass Factory on top.*
>
> *To lead off the evening's festivities, the sponsor invited the talented Band of the Light Brigade from Racine. The group fielded approximately 90 members and looked sharp in their green, white and yellow uniforms. Their total membership is greater than the combined*

Kilts and Racine Scouts organizations who both performed tonight as well.

The Wausau Story is into their second year of competition after a few years of being inactive. They're small, but they have a very enjoyable production. A few more familiar tunes might help their efforts, though. Tonight they scored 20.45 for fourth.

The Kilts have improved dramatically in the last three weeks since their 1982 debut. They've dropped Twilight Tones and cleaned up their execution in all areas. The size has also climbed a bit. They had 50 members in the show. Third place earned them 22.65.

The Pioneer is the nice surprise of the midwest this year. They have a rather conservative show compared to past offerings, but it is highly entertaining and very well performed. They too suffer from size with only about 60 members, but they make up for it in good music, a well-designed drill and enthusiasm for what they are performing. The corps had hoped to overtake the Sagainaires this evening, but fell short to take home second place and 44.40 points.

The Saginaires scooped up the first place honors with a 47.90 and caption wins in drums (by 2.8 over Pioneer) and GE (1.4 over Pioneer). The show is very subdued this year. Enthusiasm for the program is lacking, at least at this point in the season. They have size (around 100) and they definitely have the talent, but so far they aren't making the best of it.

Winning their first contest in the Midwest, the Ohio Brass Factory easily defeated the Spirit of '76 in every caption except M&M. New uniforms certainly gave the corps the look of a major organization. It's a take-off on the Blue Devils' look in lime green with trim in red, gold, black and white. Fielding over 90 members, the corps appeared to be making very good progress toward achieving DCA finalist status on Labor Day. There was a bit of humor tonight as one member had trouble with his cumberbund and it became a game as to how long it would take to slip down past his hips and fall to the ground. When it finally did he stepped out of it and crowd attention returned to the corps proper. A huge margin in GE of five points set the tone for their win over Spirit of '76. However, the other captions showed only slight margins (.6 in percussion and .7 in brass). First place was good for 34.60 points in the senior portion of the show.

Spirit of '76 featured lots of big band charts and they're played quite nicely by the hornline of 24. Size definitely hurts the overall impression, but the membership displays lots of excitement for what they're doing on the field. One of the drum majors did quite a bit of cutting up beside, in front of and behind various soloists. Two members, a baritone and a soprano, were particularly good in solo spots during the show. They're also planning to attend DCA in Allentown on Labor Day. Second place tonight, brought Spirit a score of 29.05.

An exhibition was performed during tabulation of the scores by the Racine Scouts.

They were quite small in numbers, only 35 members, but it was great to see them on the field again. Their performance was dedicated to the lady who made their new set of uniforms. For several years the corps has worn white shirts and black pants with a red sash. Now they have returned to the same basic uniform the corps wore during the sixties, a blue jacket with white sash and the explorer scout emblem on the sash. They also had the old chrome helmets that earned their nickname years ago, the Chromedomes. More work will yield better results competitively, Right now the show isn't finished and members weren't confident about the music or the drill.

The Drum Corps Midwest show had a full panel of judges including: Tim Guare, J. Lahmann, J. Titzkowski and Gary Czapinski on M&M, T. Olshanski, Joe Kluber and Stan Finck on percussion and R. Janusiak, Terry Anderegg and Ben Kordus on brass.

A big crowd was on hand to usher in the July 4th holiday and enjoy an evening of drum corps.

—Drum Corps World, *July 16, 1982*

August 6, 1982—One Night in August

This was the Troopers' thirteenth appearance and its seventh and last win in Horlick Field. The Troopers took fourteenth in DCI prelims, the Colts twenty-fourth. The show had six drum corps from five states.

August 6, 1982—One Night in August

1. 76.9 Troopers
2. 68.3 Colts
3. 64.2 Saginaires
4. 53.3 Blue Stars
5. 48.4 Royal Grenadiers
6. 34.6 Vaqueros

1983–1985

The year 1983 was the first since 1953 that Horlick Field did not host a drum and bugle corps show. Horlick Field had hosted at least one drum and bugle corps show a year for twenty-nine straight years, from 1954 to 1982. There were no drum and bugle corps shows in Horlick Field in 1983, 1984 or 1985. Spirit of '76 hosted its annual shows in Pershing Park on Racine's lakeshore in those years.

JULY 3, 1986—SPECTACULAR

After three years of weak, poorly attended drum corps shows held in Pershing Park on the lakefront in Racine, the Spirit of '76 made a strong effort to put together and promote a high-quality drum corps show in 1986 and brought its annual show back to Horlick Field. For the first time in years, it bought ads in the *Racine Journal Times* to promote the contest, and for the first time ever, it bought ads in *Drum Corps World*.

The show had two DCI championship finalists, Phantom Regiment and the Troopers, and the Geneseo Knights, a big, entertaining unit that finished twenty-first at DCI prelims. Overall, the show had nine drum corps from three states. It was the best show in six years. It was the first of three straight years that the Troopers appeared in Horlick Field. There were two Northmen drum and bugle corps competing during this time. This Northmen was from Green Bay, Wisconsin.

Also of note, the show hosted a Kilties reunion and standstill performance. Many members of the great Kilties corps from 1964 through 1975 performed, including the Kilties' famous drum major, Scotty Paulsen.

JULY 3, 1986—SPECTACULAR

1. 81.0 Phantom Regiment D10
2. 74.9 Troopers D11
3. 65.9 Geneseo Knights
4. 43.1 Northmen
5. 38.7 Madison Junior Scouts
6. 35.4 Guardsmen

Exhibition

New Day
Racine Scouts
Spirit of '76

Celebrating our 70th Anniversary in 1986!

"Thanks for the memories"

July 3 Spectacular Drum Corps Competition

8:00 PM—Horlick Athletic Field
1648 North Memorial Drive, Racine, Wisconsin
(Corner of High Street and Memorial Drive)

Tickets $5.00 (Donation)
Price good until June 30—$6.00 at gate

Hosted by Spirit of '76 Senior Drum & Bugle Corps
Racine, Wisconsin

Drum corps in competition:

Troopers—Casper, Wyoming
Phantom Regiment—Rockford, Illinois
Knights—Geneseo, Illinois
Northmen—Green Bay, Wisconsin
Madison Junior Scouts—Madison, Wisconsin
Guardsmen—Schaumburg, Illinois

Units in exhibition:

New Day All-Girl Corps—Racine, Wisconsin
Racine Scouts—Racine, Wisconsin

Judged exhibition:

Spirit of '76 Senior Corps
Racine, Wisconsin

Mail-in coupon

Please send me ________ advance tickets.
Enclosed please find $ ________ to cover the amount of tickets I have requested at $5.00@.

Please send my tickets to:
Name ____________________
Address ____________________
City ____________________
State ____________ Zip ________

Please make check/money order payable to Spirit of '76
or call Dee at 414-631-7311 between 7:45 AM and 4:30 PM

Mail coupon to
Spirit of '76 July 3 Spectacular
Post Office Box 484
Racine, Wisconsin 53401

Ticket orders received up to June 19 will be mailed. Orders after June 19 will be held at the stadium box office.

Payment for tickets must be made prior to June 30 for advance ticket prices, otherwise the $6.00 gate ticket price will apply.

Phantom easily tops Troopers in Racine, WI
by Dr. Rosalie Sward
July 3, 1986—Racine, Wisconsin
"'Twas the night before the Fourth and all through the stand, everyone thought the return of the Kilts was just grand." Complete with a bagpiper, a nearly-full corps of Kilts alumni, most of whom marched before 1975, presented an exhibition that thrilled both the old and new drum corps fans at the Spirit of '76 Spectacular. Under the direction of Scotty Paulsen, the Kilts presented Scotland the Brave, Chattanooga Choo-Choo and Auld Lang Syne. Although the corps was not in uniform, both the Anderson plaid and the McLeod of Lewis plaid were on the field. The 16-man rifle line did some aerial work in right field, and afterward everyone was saying, "Wouldn't it be great if the Kilts would return as a senior corps?" There is the rumored possibility of a DCI exhibition.

Moving into the competition of the evening, fireworks were heard in the distance, and some spectators felt that a few scores were blown up as well.

The Phantom Regiment performed last, confident that this was their night to sparkle, and determined to put out their very best effort, which resulted in their season-high score of 81.00, with 17.10 in the ensemble brass caption, for first place. However, due to their extra difficulty, they were third in field visual (7.90) to the Troopers' 8.30 and Knights' 8.10. There has been noticeable improvement in the musicality of the Alborada. Phantom brought back many fond memories as they played Elsa's Procession to the Cathedral as their encore.

"As TV viewers tuned in to America all over the land, where Dan Rathers announced the Garfield Cadet Band," this Racine drum corps audience had their own special tribute to America from the Troopers, whose second-place score of 74.90 took a giant leap from last week's Eastern scores in the low 60s. The Troopers had to be very tired as they approached the end of their long tour with a bus breakdown, but they provided an appropriately moving close to their performance with their presentation of the colors and the red, white and blue banners which have now been moved to backfield during Battle Hymn.

No penalties for anyone tonight, including the Geneseo Knights, who are now performing without their electronic percussion equipment. Not by choice, however—they were informed that they would be disqualified if they continued to use it after the Normal, IL, show of June 22. Director Greg Neuleib had hoped that this means of sound amplification would help the Knights in the competition with corps of greater size, but many drum corps fans have felt that it didn't add that much to the show. With a score increase tonight to 65.90, the Knights may be better off without the electronics. They were in third place.

Who can forget that "neon" drum major who hopped on the podium like a kangaroo and sparkled like Liberace throughout the show in his purple sequined jacket and white gloves? The second most memorable thing about the Northmen is the versatile and talented 14-member guard, which is featured for much of the show in flag, rifle and dance segments. Fourth place, 43.10.

One minor disappointment in this years' shows to date has been the lack of competition between any of the corps. However, tonight there was a surprise at the bottom, as the Madison Jr. Scouts overtook the Guardsmen with 38.70 for fifth place to 35.40 for sixth. Both corps have very entertaining programs, and again the Jr. Scouts' equipment personnel continued to amuse the audience with their unrehearsed antics.

A post-show exhibition was provided by New Day in new flashy royal blue and white uniforms.

—Drum Corps World, *July 25, 1986*

July 3, 1987—Spectacular

In 1987, Spirit of '76 again advertised the show and invited championship-caliber drum corps to perform. This show had DCI's third-place drum corps and the seventeenth-place Troopers.

July 3, 1987—Spectacular
1. 83.5 Cavaliers..D3
2. 70.0 Troopers
3. 38.6 Northmen
4. 34.7 Madison Junior Scouts
5. 27.8 Pioneer
6. 27.5 CapitolAires

Exhibition
New Day
Racine Scouts
Spirit of '76

July 1, 1988—Spectacular

This was the best show in Horlick Field in ten years, since the 1978 Kiltie show that hosted six DCI finalists. It had the fifth- and sixth-place DCI units, the Phantom Regiment and the Cavaliers. With the rise of DCI, tours and shows were packaged, and most shows got only two or three of the top corps. Only regional championship shows in large stadiums had a full slate of championship finalists. So this was a good show in its time.

This was the first of three consecutive years that Phantom Regiment appeared and won in Horlick Field.

July 1, 1988—Spectacular

1. 78.7 Phantom Regiment D6
2. 75.8 Cavaliers D5
3. 62.9 Troopers
4. 43.7 Phantom Regiment Cadets
5. 38.3 Bandettes
6. 37.6 Guardsmen
7. 34.5 Railmen
8. 32.4 Northmen

July 3, 1989—Spectacular

Phantom Regiment, which took second at DCI championships in 1989, was the highest finishing drum and bugle corps to appear in Horlick Field in twelve years, since the 1978 Kiltie show hosted the first-place Santa Clara Vanguard and second-place Phantom Regiment. The Sky Ryders, a very entertaining corps that was a crowd favorite for years, finished fifteenth at DCI prelims. The Colts finished twenty-first and was also a strong, entertaining corps.

The Quad City Knights was a continuation of the Kewanee Black Knights/Geneseo Knights. The corps finished last in DCI Open Class prelims in 1989. The Guardsmen and Northmen failed to make Class A finals.

Celebrating our 73rd anniversary in 1989!

"Thanks for the memories"

July 3 Spectacular

Drum Corps Competition

8:00 PM -- Horlick Athletic Field

1648 North Memorial Drive, Racine, Wisconsin
(Corner of High Street and Memorial Drive)

Hosted by Spirit of '76 Senior Drum & Bugle Corps
Racine, Wisconsin

Tickets $7.00

Drum Corps in competition:

Phantom Regiment **-- Rockford, Illinois**
Sky Ryders **-- Hutchinson, Kansas**
Colts **-- Dubuque, Iowa**
Quad-City Knights **-- Bettendorf, Iowa**
Guardsmen **-- Schaumburg, Illinois**
Northmen **-- Green Bay, Wisconsin**
and others!

Please send me ____ advance tickets. Enclosed please find ____ to cover the amount of the tickets I have requested at $7.00 each.

Please send tickets to:
Name ____________________

Address ____________________

City ____________________

State __________ Zip __________

Please make check/money order payable to ***Spirit of '76***

For information call Dee at
414-631-7311 (7:45 am to 4:30 pm)
414-632-7599 (evenings)

Ticket orders received up to June 23 will be mailed. Orders after June 23 will be held at the stadium box office.

Mail coupons to:
Spirit of '76 July 3 Spectacular
Post Office Box 484
Racine, WI 53401

JULY 3, 1989—SPECTACULAR
1. 82.6 Phantom Regiment D2
2. 71.6 Sky Ryders
3. 61.8 Colts
4. 47.2 Quad City Knights
5. 36.1 Guardsmen
6. 35.3 Northmen (WI)

Exhibition
Racine Scouts

JULY 3, 1990—SPECTACULAR

This was the last of the thirty-seven annual Spectaculars that the Boys/Spirit of '76 hosted.

It was the fifth year in a row that Horlick Field hosted a good drum show, and it followed the old model. It had ten corps from five states, a senior corps and the Troopers. It had only one finalist but also had two other corps in the top twenty-five. The advertised Oakland Crusaders did not appear.

JULY 3, 1990—SPECTACULAR
1. 80.4 Phantom Regiment D4
2. 66.4 Troopers
3. 62.3 Glassmen
4. 55.4 Railmen
5. 49.6 Pioneer
6. 41.8 Expressions
7. 38.7 Phantom Regiment Cadets
8. 32.7 Chicago Vanguard senior

Exhibition
Racine Scouts
Racine Junior Scouts

1991

There were no drum and bugle corps shows in Horlick Field in 1991.

JULY 3, 1992—RACINE SCOUTS SIXTY-FIFTH ANNIVERSARY SPECIAL

After only four practices, sixty-nine former members of the Racine Scouts, including members from as far back as the 1940s, performed a standstill concert at the contest and marched in the Fourth of July parade the next day. The show hosted only five drum corps, but it was a good show. The Glassmen placed thirteenth, the Colts nineteenth and the Northern Aurora twenty-third at DCI prelims.

JULY 3, 1992—RACINE SCOUTS SIXTY-FIFTH ANNIVERSARY SPECIAL

1. 68.7 Glassmen
2. 64.9 Colts
3. 61.5 Northern Aurora
4. 56.1 Limited Edition
5. 45.3 Americanos

1993

For the second time in three years, Horlick Field did not host a drum and bugle corps show.

JULY 8, 1994—KILTIE KLASSIC

With the Boys/Spirit of '76 no longer operating and hosting shows, the Kilties Senior corps hosted the first of its annual Kiltie Klassic contests in 1994.

In a highly competitive year, Phantom took fifth at DCI Midwest but ended up third at DCI championships. Madison took sixth and Colts took twelfth. Pioneer was DCI Division II Champion, and the Americanos was DCI Division III Champion. This was the fifth and last appearance by the Kewanee/Geneseo/Quad City Knights.

July 8, 1994—Kiltie Klassic

1. 80.2 Phantom Regiment....................D3
2. 79.3 Madison Scouts....................D6
3. 71.5 Colts....................D12
4. 62.0 Pioneer
5. 53.0 Americanos
6. 50.5 Quad City Knights
7. 42.3 Phantom Regiment Cadets

Exhibition

Kilties Senior

July 7, 1995—Kiltie Klassic II

This was another good show. It had nine drum corps, two finalists and the DCI Division II champion Pioneer.

July 7, 1995—Kiltie Klassic II

1. 82.3 Madison Scouts....................D4
2. 72.3 Colts....................D9
3. 66.1 Pioneer
4. 57.4 Nite Express
5. 51.4 Blue Stars
6. 44.5 Kilties Senior
7. 39.8 Colt Cadets
8. 38.0 Phantom Regiment Cadets
9. 33.5 Racine Scouts

July 5, 1996—Kiltie Klassic Invitational

Seeing a national champion for the first time in eighteen years was a sad reminder of how far Horlick Field had fallen as a drum and bugle corps venue. In 1968 through 1970 alone, Horlick Field hosted a VFW or American Legion champion nine times.

July 5, 1996—Kiltie Klassic Invitational
1. 81.0 Cavaliers....................D4
2. 79.6 Phantom Regiment....................D1
3. 65.6 Pioneer
4. 52.7 Blue Stars
5. 49.5 Capital Sound
6. 40.8 Phantom Regiment Cadets
7. 34.4 Racine Scouts

Exhibition
Bayou City Blues
St. Joseph's of Batavia Reunion Corps
Kilties Senior

1997 and 1998

Horlick Field did not host a drum and bugle corps show in 1997 or 1998.

July 4, 1999—Kiltie Klassic

Notably, this show had three corps that had been in continuous operation for over sixty years: the Racine Scouts (1927), the Appleton Americanos (1936) and the Madison Scouts (1938). Madison and the Americanos both first appeared in Horlick Field in 1946.

July 4, 1999—Kiltie Klassic
1. 78.9 Madison Scouts....................D4
2. 57.9 Capital Sound
3. 57.7 Kilties Senior
4. 39.9 Memorial Lancers
5. 31.4 Racine Scouts

Exhibition
Americanos
Cincinnati Glory
Bayou City Blues

June 17, 2000—Music on the March

Only one drum corps in this show scored above fifty. The winning Minnesota Brass, Inc. finished fifth at DCA championships.

June 17, 2000—Music on the March
1. 57.45 Minnesota Brass, Inc. DCA5
2. 47.05 Capital Sound
3. 44.10 Blue Stars
4. 37.50 Kilties Senior
5. 26.15 Racine Scouts
6. 16.95 Joliet Kingsmen

July 4, 2000—Kiltie Klassic

Madison won its third show in its last three appearances in Horlick Field.

The year 2000 was the ninth in a row that Southwind placed in the top twenty-five at DCI championships, and in total, it would make DCI's top twenty-five for sixteen straight years without ever making finals. This year was its highest finish in that sixteen-year span: it placed thirteenth, just 0.15 out of finals.

July 4, 2000—Kiltie Klassic
1. 76.40 Madison Scouts D10
2. 68.10 Southwind
3. 67.65 Pioneer
4. 56.60 Capital Sound
5. 54.80 Americanos
6. 52.10 General Butler Vagabonds
7. 48.45 Kilties Senior
8. 34.95 Racine Scouts

Exhibition
Bayou City Blues

July 1, 2001—Kiltie Klassic

This was Phantom Regiment's thirteenth appearance in Horlick Field, tied for seventh most by any drum and bugle corps not from Racine. It was the corps' seventh win, tied for third in total victories in Horlick Field behind the Kilties and Madison Scouts. Phantom Regiment first performed in Horlick Field in 1974. Phantom Regiment placed sixth at DCI championships in 2001, and the Pioneer finished eighteenth in prelims.

July 1, 2001—Kiltie Klassic

1. 75.40 Phantom Regiment..D6
2. 54.95 Pioneer
3. 50.75 Kilties Senior
4. 38.95 Lake Erie Regiment
5. 35.00 Racine Scouts
6. 33.70 Bandettes

July 7, 2002—Kiltie Klassic

For the first time in six years, Horlick Field hosted the season's DCI champion in the Cavaliers.

The Royal Airs Alumni corps, which was thrilling crowds everywhere during the summer, played in the old stadium in which most of the members had performed in their youth. Some of them may have been reminded of the big 1967 Spectacular upset thirty-five years earlier, at which the Racine Scouts beat the Royal Airs, Des Plaines Vanguard, Troopers and Kilties.

July 7, 2002—Kiltie Klassic

1. 86.85 Cavaliers..D1
2. 68.15 Capital Regiment
3. 63.30 Capital Sound
4. 61.30 Pioneer
5. 54.85 Kilties Senior
6. 39.10 Racine Scouts
7. 33.35 Joliet Kingsmen

Exhibition

Royal Airs Alumni

2003

There were no drum and bugle corps shows in Horlick Field in 2003.

July 5, 2004—Kiltie Klassic

St. Patrick's Imperials/The Thing/Pioneer drum and bugle corps appeared for the twenty-seventh time in Horlick Field, just two behind the Madison Scouts' twenty-nine appearances. Madison first appeared in 1946. The St. Patrick's Imperials/The Thing/Pioneer organization first appeared in 1963.

July 5, 2004—Kiltie Klassic

1. 66.9 Pioneer
2. 58.1 Lake Erie Regiment
3. 54.4 Kilties Senior
4. 40.2 Bandettes
5. 40.0 Capital Sound
6. 32.9 Racine Scouts
7. 28.8 Joliet Kingsmen

July 4, 2005—Kiltie Klassic

The 2005 Kiltie Klassic was judged by "VIP Judging." Notable Racine residents worked as a panel to select the order of placement.

The show had eight drum corps from five states, but this is in no way remarkable. Where once Horlick Field had almost a monopoly on out-of-state drum corps, now every drum and bugle corps show had to have out-of-state drum corps or there would be no show. Few regional drum corps were left to fill out a show. Pioneer finished twenty-third at DCI quarterfinals, and Teal Sound placed fourth in DCI's Division II championship show.

July 4, 2005—Kiltie Klassic
VIP Judging
1. Pioneer
2. Teal Sound
3. Kilties Senior
4. Capital Sound
5. Music City Legend
6. Lake Erie Regiment
7. Gulf Coast Sound
8. Racine Scouts

2006

There were no shows in Horlick Field in 2006.

June 22, 2007—Kiltie Klassic

Madison Scouts won for the twelfth time in Horlick Field, tied with the Kilties for the most wins ever in Horlick Field. This was the Troopers' eighteenth appearance in Horlick Field.

June 22, 2007—Kiltie Klassic
All-Age
1. 61.875 Kilties Senior

Division I
1. 64.450 Madison Scouts
2. 61.250 Troopers
3. 55.700 Pioneer

Division III
1. 50.700 Capital Sound
2. 41.300 Racine Scouts

JUNE 27, 2008—KILTIE KLASSIC

Pioneer appeared for the thirtieth time in Horlick Field, tying Madison Scouts for the most appearances in Horlick Field by a corps from outside Racine. The Pioneer appeared in fifteen of the twenty-two Horlick Field drum and bugle corps shows between 1981 and 2008 and the last seven straight Horlick Field shows to date. Overall, the St. Patrick's/The Thing/Pioneer drum and bugle corps appeared in thirty of the ninety-eight Horlick Field drum and bugle corps shows to this date, and thirteen of those took place before St. Patrick's was formed. Since it was formed, the drum corps appeared in two of every five Horlick Field shows.

This was a fairly good show, with two DCI finalists and a total of seven corps from five states including New Jersey, Massachusetts, Wyoming and Texas.

This was the third appearance by the Boston Crusaders and the nineteenth appearance by the Troopers. Only Racine drum corps and the Wisconsin-based Madison Scouts and Pioneer appeared in Horlick Field more than the Troopers.

JUNE 27, 2008—KILTIE KLASSIC

All-Age

1. 66.6 Kilties All-age

Open Class

1. 63.6 Revolution
2. 55.5 Racine Scouts

World Class

1. 77.4 The Cadets..D5
2. 73.8 Boston Crusaders..D10
3. 65.4 Troopers
4. 58.8 Pioneer

2009–2012

There were no shows held in Horlick Field between 2009 and 2012.

August 3, 2013—Kiltie Klassic

Kilties All-age drum and bugle corps, Horlick Field, August 3, 2013. *Photo by author.*

For the first time in five years, Horlick Field hosted the Kiltie Klassic for this Alumni Celebration. It was the ninety-ninth drum corps show in Horlick Field history. It was Govenaires' third time in Horlick Field and its first win.

The grandstands had been remodeled in 2006, reducing the seating by thousands. The grandstands used to go from end zone to end zone, stood many rows higher and would have filled the picture above side to side.

August 3, 2013—Kiltie Klassic

Class A

1. 81.65 Govenaires
2. 74.65 Cincinnati Tradition

Open

1. 90.15 Minnesota Brass, Inc.
2. 75.50 Kilties All-age

Exhibition

Chops, Inc.

Appendix

Some Horlick Athletic Field Facts

- Horlick Field hosted at least one drum corps show each year for twenty-nine straight years (1954–82).
- Of the three non-Racine drum and bugle corps that appeared the most in Horlick Field, the first was from 20 miles away; the second was from 90 miles away; and the third, the Troopers, was from 1,100 miles away.
- Kilties had the most appearances in Horlick Field in a drum corps show (sixty-six).
- The Kilties and the Madison Scouts tied for the most wins (twelve) in Horlick Field.
- Madison Scouts and St. Patrick's/Pioneer each appeared in Horlick Field thirty times, the most by a corps from outside Racine.
- Fifty-three different drum and bugle corps won competitions in Horlick Field.
- Only nineteen drum and bugle corps won more than one competition in Horlick Field.
- The Racine Scouts won only one contest in Horlick Field.
- The Racine Legion/Boys of '76 won only one contest in Horlick Field.

- Twelve different Racine drum and bugle corps are known to have appeared in Horlick Field (it is likely that up to four more Racine drum corps appeared in Horlick Field but were not recorded).
- The Maumee Demons appeared only three times and won all three contests.

List of Horlick Athletic Field Drum and Bugle Corps Shows

1	June 24, 1939	VFW State
2	September 13, 1941	Racine Legion (Boys of '76) Show
3	August 3, 1946	American Legion State
4	June 1, 1952	Twenty-fifth Anniversary free show
5	July 5, 1952	Giant Midwest Drum Corps Contest
6	June 26, 1954	State VFW Show
7	July 2, 1955	Fourth Annual Midwest Drum Corps Contest
8	July 3, 1956	Fifth Annual Midwest Drum Corps Contest
9	July 3, 1957	Seventh Annual Midwest Drum Corps Contest
10	July 3, 1958	Midwest Drum and Bugle Corps Contest
11	July 3, 1959	Eighth Annual Goodwill Drum Corps Contest
12	July 3, 1960	1960 Goodwill Spectacular
13	July 1, 1961	Twelfth Annual Goodwill Spectacular
14	July 3, 1962	Goodwill Spectacular
15	August 11, 1962	Music on the March
16	September 1, 1962	Senior Spectacular

17	July 3, 1963	Goodwill Spectacular
18	August 11, 1963	Music on the March
19	August 31, 1963	Spectacular II
20	July 3, 1964	East-West Spectacular
21	July 29, 1964	Roland Olson Memorial Concert
22	August 8, 1964	Music on the March
23	June 7, 1965	Drum Corps Day
24	July 4, 1965	Goodwill Spectacular
25	August 14, 1965	Music on the March
26	September 5, 1965	First All-Midwest Senior Championship
27	July 3, 1966	Goodwill Spectacular
28	August 13, 1966	Music on the March
29	July 3, 1967	Goodwill Spectacular
30	August 5, 1967	Music on the March
31	July 3, 1968	Goodwill Spectacular
32	August 10, 1968	Music on the March
33	May 31, 1969	Kiltie Kadet Show
34	July 3, 1969	Goodwill Spectacular
35	August 9, 1969	Music on the March
36	August 30, 1969	Labor Day Drums
37	May 31, 1970	Kiltie Kadet Show
38	July 3, 1970	Goodwill Spectacular
39	August 8, 1970	Music on the March
40	September 5, 1970	Labor Day Spectacle
41	July 3, 1971	Goodwill Spectacular
42	August 7, 1971	Music on the March
43	July 3, 1972	Goodwill Spectacular
44	July 29, 1972	Music on the March

45	August 19, 1972	Senior Spectacular
46	July 3, 1973	Spectacular
47	August 15, 1973	DCI preview
48	July 3, 1974	Goodwill Spectacular
49	July 13, 1974	Music on the March
50	July 21, 1974	Horns-a-Plenty
51	July 28, 1974	Capital of Corps Championship
52	July 3, 1975	Goodwill Spectacular
53	July 11, 1975	Music on the March
54	August 3, 1975	Capital of Corps Championship
55	August 9, 1975	Belle City Drum Corps "75"
56	July 3, 1976	Twenty-fifth Annual Spectacular
57	July 11, 1976	Music on the March
58	July 18, 1976	Belle City Drum Corps "76"
59	August 8, 1976	Brigadoon
60	August 8, 1976	Capital of Corps Championship
61	July 3, 1977	Spectacular
62	July 17, 1977	Belle City Drum Corps "77"
63	August 7, 1977	Brigadoon
64	August 7, 1977	Capital of Corps Championship
65	August 20, 1977	Music on the March
66	August 27, 1977	Mid-States Senior Association Championship Show
67	June 24, 1978	VFW State
68	July 3, 1978	Spectacular
69	July 16, 1978	Cadet Corps International Contest
70	July 16, 1978	Capital of Corps Championship
71	June 23, 1979	Music On the March
72	July 13, 1979	Capital of Corps Championship

73	July 3, 1980	Fourth Fest Spectacular
74	July 13, 1980	Brigadoon
75	July 13, 1980	Scottish Supersound
76	August 23, 1980	Cadet Corps International Championships
77	July 4, 1981	Fourth Fest Spectacular
78	August 7, 1981	One Night in August
79	July 3, 1982	Spectacular
80	August 6, 1982	One Night in August
81	July 3, 1986	Spectacular
82	July 3, 1987	Spectacular
83	July 1, 1988	Spectacular
84	July 3, 1989	Spectacular
85	July 3, 1990	Spectacular
86	July 3, 1992	Racine Scouts Sixty-fifth Anniversary Show
87	July 3, 1994	Kiltie Klassic
88	July 3, 1995	Kiltie Klassic II
89	July 5, 1996	Kiltie Klassic Invitational
90	July 4, 1999	Kiltie Klassic
91	June 17, 2000	Music on the March
92	July 4, 2000	Kiltie Klassic
93	July 1, 2001	Kiltie Klassic
94	July 7, 2002	Kiltie Klassic
95	July 5, 2004	Kiltie Klassic
96	July 4, 2005	Kiltie Klassic
97	June 22, 2007	Kiltie Klassic
98	June 27, 2008	Kiltie Klassic
99	August 3, 2013	Kiltie Klassic

List of Rainouts

1	July 3, 1953	Giant Midwest Drum Corps Contest
2	June 16, 1973	Music on the March
3	July 3, 1979	Goodwill Spectacular

Number of Times Each Corps Appeared in Horlick Athletic Field

Racine Units

66	Kilties
65	Racine Scouts
56	Boys of '76/Spirit of '76
48	Kiltie Kadets
31	Racine Junior Scouts
25	AmbassaDears/New Day
13	Kilties Senior/All-age
6	New Dawn
3	Armenian Youth
3	Roma Lodge
1	Belle City
1	Racine Rookie Scouts

Visiting Units

30	Imperials of St. Patrick/Pioneer
30	Madison Scouts
19	Troopers
17	Cavaliers
16	Blue Stars

Pioneer publicity photo, 2013. *Courtesy of the Pioneer drum and bugle corps.*

14	Mercury Thunderbolts
13	Appleton SAL/Americanos
13	Norwood Park/Skokie Imperials
13	Phantom Regiment
12	Guardsmen
12	Madison Junior Scouts
11	Minnesota Brass, Inc.
10	Mel Tierney/Des Plaines/Skokie/Chicago Vanguard
9	Mariners
8	Capital Sound
8	Colt 45s/Colts
8	Phantom Regiment Cadets
7	Kenosha Kingsmen
7	Kenosha Queensmen
7	Santa Clara Vanguard
7	Spirit of St. Louis
6	St. Matthias Cadets

6	St. Paul Scouts
5	Anaheim Kingsmen
5	Cavalier Cadets
5	Kewanee/Geneseo/Quad City Knights
5	Royal Airs
4	Marion Cadets
4	Marquis
4	Militaires
4	Northmen
4	Oshkosh Warriors
4	Skokie Indians
4	Stardusters
4	St. Matthias Prep
4	Vaqueros
3	Bandettes
3	Bayou City Blues
3	Belles of St. Mary's
3	Boston Crusaders
3	Bridgemen (St. Andrew's Bridgemen)
3	CapitolAire Petites
3	CapitolAires
3	Chicago Connection
3	Hamm's Indians
3	Imperial Cadets
3	Joliet Kingsmen
3	Kewanee Black Knights Senior
3	Lake Erie Regiment
3	Maumee Demons
3	Mercy High School All-girl
3	Royal Grenadiers

3	Saginaires
3	Sky Ryders
3	Toronto Optimists
3	Velvet Knights
3	Wausau Story
2	Austin Grenadiers
2	Belleville Black Knights
2	Blue Devils
2	Cedar Rapids Grenadiers
2	Chordaliers
2	Colt Cadets
2	Cudworth SAL
2	Edison Lamplighters
2	Evanston Lancers
2	Fort Dodge Lancers
2	Fox Valley Raiders
2	Gladiators
2	Glassmen
2	Govenaires
2	Guardsmen Cadets
2	Ishpeming Blue Notes
2	LaSalle Cadets
2	Los Charros
2	Maple City Cadets
2	Memorial Lancers
2	Men of Brass senior
2	Nisei Ambassadors
2	Northernaires
2	Railmen
2	Scarlet Knights

2	Seattle Imperials
2	Sentinels/Bellevue Washington
2	Starlites
2	St. Gregory's Crusaders
2	32nd Hussars
2	Wausau Pages
2	West Bend Patriots
1	American Woodman Cadets
1	Argonne Rebels
1	Bellefontaine Angels
1	Belleville Crusaders
1	Bendix Aviation Post
1	Bleu Raeders
1	Blue Knights
1	Blue Rock
1	The Cadets
1	Capital Regiment
1	Cedar Rapids Cadets
1	Charles Hagestrom Post
1	Charles Roth Post 692
1	Chevaliers of Waterloo
1	Chicago Vanguard Senior
1	Chops, Inc.
1	Cincinnati Glory
1	Cincinnati Tradition
1	Cleveland Caballeros
1	Colonels
1	Commonwealth Edison
1	Conquistadors
1	Cornwall Post

1	Crossmen
1	Crusader-Gladiators
1	Curtis O. Reddin Post 210
1	Custer's Brigade
1	Dutch Boy Cadets
1	Emerald Knights
1	Etobicoke Crusaders
1	Expressions
1	First Canadian Regiment
1	Fond du Lac Post
1	Gary Memorial Post 232
1	General Butler Vagabonds
1	General George Bell Corps
1	Gulf Coast Sound
1	Hawthorne Caballeros
1	Henry J. Schaefer VFW (Schaefer Ladies)
1	Janesville
1	Kenosha Shoreliners
1	Kenosha Squires
1	Kingston Indians
1	La Porte Lancers
1	Limited Edition
1	Long Island Kingsmen
1	Marching Ambassadors
1	Melin Romer Post 728
1	Men of Brass junior
1	Meuli-Kilian Unit 77, Chippewa Falls All-girl
1	Mounties
1	Music City Legend
1	Nee-Hi's

1	Nite Express
1	Northern Aurora
1	Ohio Brass Factory
1	Overseas Drum and Bugle Corps
1	Page Park Cadets
1	Peoria Post 2
1	Pittsburgh Rockets
1	Port Washington Legion
1	Princemen, Canada
1	Princemen, San Mateo, California
1	Queen City Cadets
1	Revolution
1	Rhinelander
1	River Falls Post 121
1	Rochester Crusaders
1	Royal Airs Alumni
1	Royal Crusaders
1	Royals
1	Sandusky Eaglettes
1	Sarnia Sertomanaires
1	Sharvin Red Jackets
1	Sheboygan
1	Silver Spectrum
1	Southwind
1	Spartans
1	Spirit of Atlanta
1	Square Post 232
1	Statesmen
1	St. Brendan's Patriots
1	St. Clair Shores Vanguard

1	St. Francis Sancians
1	St. Johns All-girl
1	St. Joseph's of Batavia
1	St. Joseph's of Batavia Reunion Corps
1	St. Raphael's Golden Buccaneers
1	St. Rita's Brassmen
1	Sundowners
1	Teal Sound
1	Thomas Rooney VFW Post 1530
1	Trailblazers
1	Valiant Knights
1	Windjammers
1	Winfield Scott Rebels
1	Wolf Olson VFW Post 1230

NUMBER OF WINS IN HORLICK ATHLETIC FIELD

12	Kilties
12	Madison Scouts
7	Cavaliers
7	Kiltie Kadets
7	Minnesota Brass, Inc.
7	Phantom Regiment
7	Troopers
3	Blue Stars
3	Maumee Demons
2	Bridgemen
2	Des Plaines Vanguard

2	Kilties Senior Corps
2	Madison Junior Scouts
2	Marion Cadets
2	Norwood Park Imperials
2	Pioneer
2	Santa Clara Vanguard
2	Skokie Indians
2	Spirit of St. Louis
1	AmbassaDears
1	Anaheim Kingsmen
1	Austin Grenadiers
1	Blue Devils
1	Boston Crusaders
1	Boys of '76
1	The Cadets
1	Capital Sound
1	Capitolaires
1	Cornwall Post
1	Cudworth SAL
1	Curtis O. Reddin Post 210
1	Fort Dodge Lancers
1	Glassmen
1	Govenaires
1	Guardsmen
1	Henry J. Schaefer VFW (Schaefer Ladies)
1	Kenosha Shoreliners
1	LaSalle Cadets
1	Marching Ambassadors
1	Memorial Lancers, St. Louis
1	Meuli-Kilian Unit 77, Chippewa Falls All-girl

1	Nisei Ambassadors
1	Ohio Brass Factory
1	Oshkosh Warriors
1	Our Lady of Mercy All-girl
1	Overseas Drum and Bugle Corps
1	Racine Scouts
1	Revolution
1	River Falls Post 121
1	Saginaires
1	Teal Sound
1	Thunderbolts
1	Wolf Olson VFW Post 1230

BIGGEST SHOWS IN HORLICK ATHLETIC FIELD HISTORY

Contests That Hosted the Top Four VFW/DCI Drum and Bugle Corps

July 3, 1964—East-West Spectacular

Kilties	V1
Royal Airs	V2
Cavaliers	V3
Boston Crusaders	V4

August 8, 1976—Capital of Corps Championship

Blue Devils	D1
Madison Scouts	D2
Santa Clara Vanguard	D3
Phantom Regiment	D4

Contests That Hosted the Top Three VFW/DCI Drum and Bugle Corps

July 3, 1963—Goodwill Spectacular

Cavaliers	V1
Troopers	V2
Racine Scouts	V3

July 3, 1968—Goodwill Spectacular

Kilties	V1
Cavaliers	V2
Troopers	V3

July 3, 1969—Goodwill Spectacular

Kilties	V1
Cavaliers	V2 A1
Troopers	V3 A2

July 28, 1974—Capital of Corps Championship

Santa Clara Vanguard	D1
Madison Scouts	D2
Anaheim Kingsmen	D3

August 3, 1975—Capital of Corps

Madison Scouts	D1
Santa Clara Vanguard	D2
Blue Devils	D3

Contests with Seven Championship Finalist Drum and Bugle Corps

July 3, 1962—Goodwill Spectacular

Cavaliers	V1
Royal Airs	V2 A2
Madison Scouts	V6
Norwood Park Imperials	V7
Kilties	V11
Racine Scouts	V12
Boys of '76	A2

August 10, 1968—Music on the March

Kilties	V1
Troopers	V3
Des Plaines Vanguard	V4
Blue Stars	V8
Racine Scouts	V9
Norwood Park Imperials	V12
Boys of '76	A2

August 9, 1969—Music on the March

Kilties	V1
Troopers	V3 A2
Des Plaines Vanguard	V6
Blue Stars	V7
Anaheim Kingsmen	V9 A4
Boys of '76	A4
Racine Scouts	A8

August 19, 1972—Senior Spectacular

Hawthorne Caballeros	DCA1
Rochester Crusaders	DCA4
Pittsburgh Rockets	DCA10
Blue Stars	D2
Santa Clara Vanguard	D3
Kilties	D8
St. Andrew's Bridgemen	D11

Contests with Six Championship Finalist Drum and Bugle Corps

July 3, 1960—Spectacular

Skokie Indians	A3
Boys of '76	A6
Kewanee Black Knights	A7
Lamplighters	A9 V2
Spirit of St. Louis	A10
Kilties	V9

July 3, 1964—East-West Spectacular

Kilties	V1
Royal Airs	V2
Cavaliers	V3
Boston Crusaders	V4
Troopers	V11
Boys of '76	A3

July 3, 1967—Goodwill Spectacular

Troopers	V2
Des Plaines Vanguard	V3
Royal Airs	V4
Kilties	V5
Racine Scouts	V6
Belleville Crusaders (Millstadt)	V8

July 3, 1968—Goodwill Spectacular

Kilties	V1
Cavaliers	V2
Troopers	V3
Royal Airs	V5
Racine Scouts	V9
Stardusters	A3

August 3, 1975—Capital of Corps Championship

Madison Scouts	D1
Santa Clara Vanguard	D2
Blue Devils	D3
Blue Stars	D5
Kilties	D7
Cavaliers	D8

August 8, 1976—Capital of Corps Championship

Blue Devils	D1
Madison Scouts	D2
Santa Clara Vanguard	D3

Phantom Regiment	D4
Cavaliers	D7
Etobicoke Crusaders	D8

July 16, 1978—Capital of Corps Championship

Santa Clara Vanguard	D1
Phantom Regiment	D2
Spirit of Atlanta	D6
Crossmen	D9
Guardsmen	D11
Kilties	D12

Index

A

AmbassaDears 104, 106, 108, 110, 116, 119, 123, 126, 128, 138, 140, 143, 145, 149, 152, 155, 158, 166
Americanos 27, 28, 45, 58, 61, 64, 148, 175, 180, 185, 206, 220, 222, 223
American Woodman Cadets 111
Anaheim Kingsmen 13, 137, 142, 151, 153, 169, 177
Argonne Rebels 167
Armenian Youth 20, 22, 43, 48, 54
Audubon Bon Bons 175
Austin Grenadiers 48, 55

B

Bandettes 217, 224, 225
Bayou City Blues 222, 223
beer 63, 88, 94, 111, 204
Belle City 20, 22, 27, 33
Bellefontaine Angels 66
Belles of St. Mary's 110, 119, 176
Belleville Black Knights 157, 165, 167
Belleville Crusaders
aka Millstadt Crusaders 123
Bendix Aviation Post 27
"big time, the" 13, 99, 149
Bleu Raeders 158
Blue Devils 182, 188
Blue Knights 198
Blue Rock 175
Blue Stars 126, 132, 143, 145, 148, 151, 161, 165, 182, 186, 198, 209, 212, 221, 222, 223
Borck, David 111
Boston Crusaders 13, 98, 102, 204, 227
Boys of '76 18, 22, 24, 27, 30, 46, 51, 55, 57, 58, 61, 66, 68, 75, 78, 82, 88, 90, 92, 98, 103, 104, 108, 113, 116, 123, 128, 132, 140, 143, 145, 149, 155, 156, 158, 161, 165, 175, 180, 219
Bridgemen 193, 205

C

Cadets, The 227
Capital Regiment 224
Capital Sound 222, 223, 224, 225, 226

CapitolAire Petites 176, 183, 187
CapitolAires 175, 198, 216
Cavalier Cadets 183, 193, 200, 206, 208
Cavaliers 45, 57, 58, 64, 75, 88, 98, 128, 140, 178, 182, 188, 194, 208, 216, 217, 222, 224
Cedar Rapids Cadets 104
Cedar Rapids Grenadiers 110, 119
Charles Hagestrom Post, Wisconsin Rapids 27
Charles Roth Post 692 30
Chevaliers of Waterloo 110
Chicago Connection 195, 198, 206
Chicago Vanguard 186
Chicago Vanguard senior 219
Chippewa Falls All-girl 28
Chops, Inc. 228
Chordaliers 90, 110
Cincinnati Glory 222
Cincinnati Tradition 228
Cleveland Caballeros 192
Colonels 192
Colt Cadets 200, 221
Colts 138, 186, 209, 212, 219, 220, 221
Commonwealth Edison 45, 51
Conquistadors 199
Cornwall SAL 27
Crossmen 200, 209
Crusader-Gladiators 148
Cudworth SAL 25, 27, 28
Curtis O. Reddin Post 210, Danville, IL 30
Custer's Brigade 104, 133

D

Dadian, Charles 110
Des Plaines Vanguard 61, 123, 132, 143, 151, 158, 186
Dowling, Joseph F. 99
Downey, Wayne 149
Drum Corps World 98, 212, 216
Dutch Boy Cadets 167

E

Eau Claire Boys 198
Eau Claire Boy Scouts 198
Edison Lamplighters 45, 66, 68
Elks Youth Band 14, 54, 57, 60, 84, 102, 104, 106, 130, 140, 158
Emerald Knights 208
Emmons, Pete 88
Etobicoke Crusaders 187, 189
Evanston Lancers 48, 57
Expressions 219

F

Fennell, George D. 19, 167
First Canadian Regiment 206
Fond du Lac Post 30
Fort Dodge Lancers 119, 126
Fox Valley Raiders 180, 187

G

Garfield Cadets 77, 97
Gary Memorial Post 232 30
General Butler Vagabonds 223
General George Bell 46
Geneseo Knights 158, 192, 213, 217, 220
Gladiators 55, 110
Glassmen 219, 220
Govenaires 195, 228
Guardsmen 110, 138, 148, 186, 194, 200, 205, 209, 210, 213, 217, 219
Guardsmen Cadets 187, 193
Gulf Coast Sound 226

H

Hamm's Indians 45, 82, 92, 113
Hardy, Gerald 159
Hawthorne Caballeros 79, 159, 161
Henry J. Schaefer VFW Post 2925 55
Holy Name drum and bugle corps 17
Horlick, William 17, 19, 23

I

Imperial Cadets 183, 187, 193
Ishpeming Blue Notes 111, 178

J

Jackson Raiders 133
Janesville 24
Johansson, Vern 101
Joliet Kingsmen 223, 224, 225

K

Kaufman, Mike 125
Kenosha Kingsmen 68, 82, 92, 105, 106, 108, 113, 116
Kenosha Queensmen 110, 116, 119, 128, 140, 143, 145, 148
Kenosha Shoreliners 110
Kenosha Squires 143
Kewanee Black Knights junior 159, 217, 220
Kewanee Black Knights senior 66, 68, 82
Kiltie Kadets 75, 78, 82, 88, 90, 92, 103, 104, 106, 110, 116, 119, 126, 128, 140, 143, 149, 152, 155, 158, 167, 174, 175, 176, 178, 180, 182, 186, 187, 188, 189, 192, 193, 194, 195, 199, 200, 204, 205, 206, 208, 209, 210
Kilties 20, 22, 27, 28, 34, 48, 51, 55, 57, 58, 60, 61, 64, 66, 68, 75, 78, 81, 83, 88, 90, 92, 98, 103, 104, 106, 108, 115, 116, 119, 123, 126, 128, 132, 140, 142, 145, 149, 151, 152, 155, 156, 158, 159, 161, 165, 167, 169, 174, 175, 178, 180, 182, 186, 188, 189, 192, 193, 194, 198, 200, 205, 210, 213
Kilties All-age 227, 228
Kilties Senior 220, 221, 222, 223, 224, 225, 226
Kingston Indians 151

L

Lake Erie Regiment 224, 225, 226
L'Anse Golden Eagles 177
La Porte Lancers 51
LaSalle Cadets 126, 132
Limited Edition 220
Logan Square 186
Long Island Kingsmen 156
Los Charros 206, 208

M

Madison Junior Scouts 90, 104, 119, 126, 175, 176, 193, 200, 206, 208, 213, 216
Madison Scouts 28, 46, 55, 57, 58, 61, 75, 78, 81, 88, 90, 98, 104, 108, 115, 116, 119, 123, 126, 132, 145, 152, 178, 182, 188, 194, 198, 221, 222, 223, 226
Maple City Cadets 78, 80, 90
Marching Ambassadors 45, 68
Mariners 128, 145, 152, 155, 156, 159, 161, 174, 175
Marion Cadets 78, 80, 165, 187, 192
Marquis 159, 180, 186, 192
Martin, C.F. 77
Maumee Demons 105, 108, 113, 116
Melin Romer Post 728 30
Mel Tierney 48, 133, 186
Memorial Lancers 204, 222
Memphis Blues Brass Band 206
Men of Brass junior 183
Men of Brass senior 105, 108, 113
Mercury Thunderbolts 45, 57, 58, 61, 64, 78, 81, 90, 104, 110, 138, 149, 152, 192, 204
Mercy High School All-girl 48, 92, 138
Meuli-Kilian Unit 77 28
Militaires 58, 92, 148
Minnesota Brass, Inc. 161, 180, 186, 192, 195, 198, 204, 206, 209, 223, 228
Morton Grove Cougars 133
Morton Grove Spartans 98, 133

Mounties 180
Munising Silver Echoes 177
Music City Legend 226

N

Nee-Hi's 138
New Dawn 175, 176, 180, 182, 187, 192
New Day 167, 174, 176, 186, 187, 192, 213, 216
Nisei Ambassadors 104, 183
Nite Express 221
Norman, Ken 94
Northernaires 111, 126, 177
Northern Aurora 220
Northmen 213, 216, 217
Norwood Park Imperials 48, 55, 57, 61, 64, 75, 88, 98, 111, 115, 119, 132

O

Ohio Brass Factory 210
Olson, Roland 102
Ontonagon Mountaineers 177
Oshkosh Warriors 110, 148, 155, 159
Ott, Jim 200
Overseas Drum and Bugle Corps 24

P

Page Park Cadets 155
PAL Cadets 97
Paulsen, Scotty 213
Peashey, Tom 163
Peoria Post 2 30
Phantom Regiment 175, 180, 188, 194, 200, 208, 213, 217, 219, 221, 222, 224
Phantom Regiment Cadets 188, 193, 200, 208, 217, 219, 221, 222
Pioneer 173, 175, 186, 188, 198, 208, 209, 210, 216, 219, 221, 222, 223, 224, 225, 226, 227
Pittsburgh Rockets 161
Port Washington Legion 51, 53
Princemen, Canada 183
Princemen, Pinole, CA 13, 140

Q

Quad City Knights 159, 219, 221
Queen City Cadets 174

R

Racine Belles 19, 34, 36, 42
Racine Junior Scouts 64, 75, 78, 88, 90, 92, 103, 104, 106, 108, 111, 116, 119, 123, 126, 128, 132, 138, 140, 143, 149, 151, 155, 156, 158, 159, 165, 167, 174, 176, 180, 219
Racine Legion 17, 18, 19, 22, 23, 24, 30, 46, 51
Racine Raiders 63, 69
Racine Rookie Scouts 104
Racine Scouts 22, 27, 28, 48, 55, 58, 61, 64, 66, 68, 75, 78, 88, 90, 103, 104, 106, 111, 115, 116, 119, 121, 126, 128, 132, 140, 143, 145, 148, 149, 151, 152, 155, 156, 158, 159, 161, 165, 175, 180, 186, 194, 206, 208, 209, 213, 216, 219, 220, 221, 222, 223, 224, 225, 226, 227
Railmen 217, 219
Reception Line, the 94
Revolution 227
Rhinelander 30
Richards, Dave 58, 147
Richmond, Cliff 80
River Falls Post 121 28
Rochester Crusaders 161, 162
Roma Lodge 22, 32
Royal Airs 75, 88, 98, 121, 128
Royal Airs Alumni 224
Royal Crusaders 180
Royal Grenadiers 208, 210, 212
Royals 152
Royer, Gale 149

S

Saginaires 208, 210, 212
Sanchez, Fred 149
Sandusky Eaglettes 119
Sanford, Fred 88
Santa Clara Vanguard 13, 143, 148, 161, 178, 182, 188, 200
Sarnia Sertomanaires 119
Scarlet Knights 180, 199
Schaefer Ladies 55
Schlecta, Tony 106
Schulte, Frederick 27
Seattle Imperials 156, 210
Sentinels 13, 132, 155
Sharvin Red Jackets 51
Sheboygan 24
Silver Spectrum 204
Skokie Imperials 174, 187
Skokie Indians 45, 51, 66, 82, 92
Skokie Vanguard 104, 124
Sky Ryders 13, 111, 155, 219
Southwind 223
Spirit of '76 186, 192, 195, 204, 206, 209, 210, 213, 216, 219
Spirit of Atlanta 200
Spirit of St. Louis 45, 66, 68, 82, 92, 108, 113, 116
Square Post 232 27, 30
St. Andrew's Bridgemen 161, 193
St. Andrew's Hornets 133
Stardusters 13, 110, 123, 128, 155
Starlites 58, 90, 92
Statesmen 210
St. Brendan's Patriots 138
St. Clair Shores Vanguard 113
St. Francis Sancians 143
St. Gregory's Crusaders 110, 119
St. John's All-girl 158
St. Joseph's of Batavia 13, 77, 78, 80
St. Joseph's of Batavia Reunion Corps 222
St. Matthias Cadets 78, 81, 82, 90, 104, 111, 116
St. Matthias Preps 90, 104, 110, 126
St. Michael's Chi-Angels 133
St. Patrick's Imperials 90, 104, 110, 140, 148, 149, 152, 155, 161, 198, 227
St. Paul Scouts 110, 119, 151, 156, 158, 159
St. Raphael's Golden Buccaneers 13, 77, 78, 80
St. Rita's Brassmen 143
St. Vincent's Cadets 79
Sullivan, John 101
Sundowners 198

T

Teal Sound 226
Thing, the 174
32nd Division Veteran's drum and bugle corps 19
32nd Hussars 151, 159
Thomas Rooney VFW Post 1530, La Crosse 55
Toronto Optimists 13, 98, 101, 167, 180, 186
Trailblazers 156
Troopers 13, 83, 88, 98, 123, 128, 132, 137, 140, 142, 147, 148, 151, 167, 180, 210, 212, 213, 216, 217, 219, 226, 227

V

Valiant Knights 192
Vaqueros 187, 209, 210, 212
Velvet Knights 13, 132, 140, 151

W

Wausau Pages 193, 200
Wausau Story 175, 197, 210
West Bend Patriots 175, 204
Windjammers 175
Winfield Scott Rebels 82
Wolf-Olson VFW Post 1230 55

About the Author

Alan Karls is a fourth-generation Racine native and was often in Horlick Athletic Field for high school football games, drum and bugle corps shows and semiprofessional football games. He was a member of the Racine Scouts and the Boys of '76 drum and bugle corps; an instructor for five Racine drum corps and three other units in Wisconsin, Illinois and Oklahoma; and a judge for Drum Corps Midwest, Pacific Coast Judges Association and Drum Corps International. He wrote championship week coverage for *Drum Corps World*, background material for a DCI championship television broadcast and album liner notes for a DCI championship recording. He holds a master's degree in communications and is a corporate writer.

Visit us at
www.historypress.net

This title is also available as an e-book